COOKBOOK

The Villa Vespa

COOKBOOK

RECIPES FROM:

"A nice little Italian Restaurant"

3/17/22

Enjoy!

Kim Vespa

Kimberly Vespa

gatekeeper press™

Columbus, Ohio

THE VILLA VESPA COOKBOOK
Recipes from "a nice little Italian Restaurant"

Published by **Gatekeeper Press**
2167 Stringtown Rd, Suite 109
Columbus, OH 43123-2989
www.GatekeeperPress.com

Illustrated Cover By Adela Bukva
Photography By Layla Wolfberg

The editorial work for this book are entirely the product of the author. Gatekeeper Press did not participate in and is not responsible for any aspect of these elements.

ISBN (paperback): 9781662920608

Contents

Introduction

This cookbook has been generations in the making.

In the early 1970s, my father, George Vespa had a dream of opening an Italian Restaurant in Lake Placid, NY. After hiring a chef from New York City's Little Italy, the Villa Vespa got its start. Throughout the years, my father made several trips to cooking schools in Europe, honing his kitchen skills and fine-tuning the recipes for the Villa Vespa. Throughout my young adult life, I worked alongside my father in the kitchen, learning the recipes and finding my own passion for food.

After the Villa Vespa closed in 1997, I opened my own takeout Italian food shop with many of the recipes from the restaurant. In addition, I jarred and sold the Villa Vespa Marinara sauce by the caseloads all over the northeastern United States.

The recipes that follow are from the kitchen at the Villa Vespa. They are classic Italian dishes made easy. Although the Villa Vespa is no longer open, now everyone can enjoy the food we've all come to love. May you use them to create great memories of your own.

Salute,

Kimberly

The Villa Vespa

"A nice little Italian Restaurant"

I can't stress enough that The Villa Vespa was not just a place to get extraordinary food. It was the restaurant where people came to get engaged, to have graduation dinners, to celebrate birthdays, and to bring a first date. It was the restaurant where you brought your kids because the atmosphere was enchanting (especially at Christmas time!). A restaurant where the kids menu was special and it told you that we love your kids.

It was the booth by the window that Horst and Edith Weber ate at so they could enjoy a meal while watching the front desk of their motel across the street. It was the 9pm cocktail hour followed by 10pm dinnertime for my dad and Charlie Hinds, after a long day in the kitchen.

For the people who worked there, it was the bridge to finishing their education, or it was the extra money they needed to raise their kids, or it was the dinner that they did not have the time or money for at home. In reality, it was the stepping stone for so many people who moved on but never forgot their start.

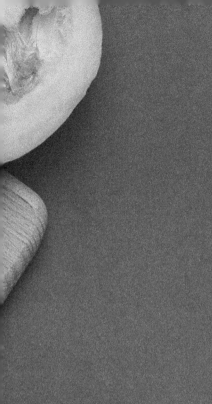

Dedication

I am dedicating this book to my parents George and Marlene Vespa.

They showed me how hard work was done. Through all the ups and downs in life they never let the challenges get to them. My sisters and I never heard them complain or feel sorry for themselves, even at times when life seemed to be falling apart. They stayed the course of life, and they built an amazing restaurant in the process.

My parents were great role models for everyone who worked "at the Villa." Many people can contribute their learned work ethic and success to the time they spent learning from my parents. I have yet to run into an old employee that doesn't have a great Marlene or George story.

They were patient when we made mistakes and gave us a chance to learn from them. My parents were some of the best life teachers. Their restaurant was a huge success and so were they.

My dad did not have the opportunity to start the restaurant until he was 50 years old. He went into this amazing adventure with the gusto and energy of a man half his age. He built a restaurant with a wonderful atmosphere and amazing food, and we served this food at the restaurant for 23 years. Now that I've put this cookbook out into the world, it is my hope that their legacy will live on, in the hearts and homes of all that have experienced these dishes.

Making the Basics

Villa Vespa Marinara Sauce

THIS IS THE SAUCE! Made with whole Italian plum tomatoes, this sauce is so incredible because of the effort and care that goes into making it. Throughout the years at the restaurant and at the store, my family and I have refused to use pre-chopped canned tomatoes. Using whole tomatoes and a particular method for deseeding them, results in a naturally sweet sauce, with a full tomato flavor.

If you take only one suggestion from me in the whole book, let it be this- do not substitute this marinara sauce for a store-bought one in the recipes that follow. This is the one. It creates the perfect base for so many of the recipes that follow. This sauce is what makes these dishes, and it is the backbone of this cookbook.

Before You Get Started

- At least ⅔ of the recipes that follow use this Villa Vespa Marinara Sauce. I highly suggest making a large batch or two of the sauce ahead of time, then storing it in the fridge or freezer. For the recipes that follow, I list "Villa Vespa Marinara Sauce" as an ingredient, but do not include it in the prep time or total cook time of the dishes. With a little forethought and planning, with your sauce already made, the majority of these recipes will be a breeze to put together.

- You can very easily double this recipe to have even more marinara sauce prepared ahead of time.

Menu Planning

Serves: 10-12 people

TIMELINE

Prep Time		30 minutes
Cook Time	+	1 hour and 40 minutes
Total Time to Serving		**2 hours, 10 minutes**

INGREDIENTS

Measurement	Ingredient	Special Instructions/Notes
90-oz	Canned Plum Tomatoes	Cento™ brand is very important
1 C.	Olive Oil	
3 C.	Yellow Onions	Diced
1 C.	Fresh Garlic	Diced
8-oz	Tomato Paste	
¼ C.	Dried basil	
½ C.	Fresh basil	Chopped
1 Tbsp.	Salt	
1 Tbsp.	Pepper	

EQUIPMENT

Name of Equipment	Special Instructions/Notes
8-11 Qt Saucepan	
Sieve or fine mesh strainer	

Directions

Step 1

Getting the tomatoes ready for sauce making- first, open the tomato can. Take one tomato out of the can, open it with your fingers, and let the seeds fall out, into the can. Place the cleaned tomato into a separate bowl. Use the same process for all the remaining tomatoes.

Step 2

When you've finished deseeding the tomatoes, transfer a handful of them onto a cutting board and dice. Place the diced tomatoes into another bowl. When all tomatoes are chopped, set the bowl aside. Set the can of tomato juice aside as well.

Step 3

In an 8-11 quart saucepan over medium heat, add the olive oil- it should cover the bottom of the pan. Add the onions and cook for 5 minutes.

Step 4

Next, stir in the garlic and cook until golden brown, about 3 minutes.

Step 5

To remove all seeds from the tomato juice, pour the can through a sieve or fine mesh strainer into the saucepan. Discard the seeds. Stir and bring to a simmer for 10 minutes.

Step 6

Stir in the chopped tomatoes and cook for 20 minutes. Then, add the tomato paste, dried basil, fresh basil, salt, and pepper, and let everything simmer for another 30 minutes.

Buon appetito!

Bolognese

A tomato sauce cooked with ground beef and hot Italian sausage. Cooking it for a long time over low heat results in a rich and savory dish. This is the basic sauce I use for the Old World Lasagna (p.146), Baked Ziti (p.149), and it can be used as a hearty substitute for the marinara sauce in the Chicken Parmigiano (p.103). Of course, it can simply be served on top of your favorite pasta for a quick, hearty, and savory meal.

Before You Get Started

- This recipe makes 5 quarts of sauce. Since it has so many ingredients and steps, I've found it is best to make a big batch and freeze some for later use.

- You can very easily double this recipe to have even more bolognese prepared ahead of time.

Menu Planning

Makes 5 quarts

Prep Time	20 minutes
Cook Time	+ 3 hours, 40 minutes
Total Time to Serving	**4 hours**

INGREDIENTS

Measurement	Ingredient	Special Instructions/Notes
90-oz	Canned Plum Tomatoes	Cento™ brand is very important
¼ C.	Olive Oil	
3 C.	Yellow Onions	Finely diced
½ C.	Garlic	Finely diced
1 lb.	Hot Italian sausage	Ground
3 lbs.	Ground beef	Preferably a 80/20 fat ratio
1 ½ C.	Good quality red wine or beef broth	
1 Tbsp.	Dried basil	
2 Tbsp	Italian Seasoning	
1 Tbsp.	Salt & Pepper	
90-oz	Italian plum tomatoes (canned)	I prefer Cento brand
1	Large Carrot	Finely diced
2	Stalks celery	Finely diced
18-oz	Tomato Paste	
1 Tbsp.	Flour	

EQUIPMENT

Name of Equipment	Special Instructions/Notes
8-11 quart saucepan	
Potato masher (optional)	

DIRECTIONS

Step 1

Getting the tomatoes ready for sauce making- first, open the tomato can. Take one tomato out of the can, open it with your fingers, and let the seeds fall out, into the can. Place the cleaned tomato into a separate bowl. Use the same process for all the remaining tomatoes.

Step 2

When you've finished deseeding the tomatoes, transfer a handful of them onto a cutting board and dice. Place the diced tomatoes into another bowl. When all tomatoes are chopped, set the bowl aside. Set the can of tomato juice aside as well.

Step 3

In an 8-11 quart saucepan over medium heat, add the olive oil- it should cover the bottom of the pan. Add the onions and cook for 5 minutes. Add the garlic and cook for 3-4 minutes. Add sausage and ground beef, cook 5 minutes more. If you have a potato masher, you can use it to break up the meat as it cooks.

Step 4

Add 1 C. wine or broth and simmer for 5 minutes. Pour the can of tomato juice through a sieve or fine mesh strainer into the saucepan. Discard the seeds. Add the dried basil, Italian seasoning, salt, and pepper. Stir the bolognese and simmer for 10 minutes.

Step 5

Add the diced carrot and celery, cook for 10 minutes. Then add the diced tomatoes. Turn the heat down to medium low and simmer for 3 hours, stirring occasionally. After one hour, add in the tomato paste.

Step 6

In a small bowl, add ½ C. wine or beef broth and 1 Tbsp flour. Whisk together, then stir into the bolognese. Allow it to cook in the sauce, at least 5 minutes. As you stir the bolognese will thicken and absorb any oil that rises to the top.

Buon appetito!

Porcini Mushroom Sauce

Toss this sauce with any type of pasta for a delicious feast. Throughout this cookbook, you can substitute the Villa Vespa Marinara Sauce for this Porcini Mushrooms sauce, to achieve a totally different dish. The dried mushrooms are pretty strong in flavor, but feel free to add extra to the mix, or toss in extra sauteed white button mushrooms if you're a real mushroom lover.

Menu Planning

Serves: 10-12 people

TIMELINE

Prep Time		30 minutes
Cook Time	+	1 hour, 30 minutes
Total Time to Serving		**2 hours**

INGREDIENTS

Measurement	Ingredient	Special Instructions/Notes
90-oz	Canned Plum Tomatoes	Cento™ brand is very important
1 C.	Olive Oil	
3 C.	Yellow Onions	Diced
1 C.	Fresh Garlic	Diced
8-oz	Tomato Paste	
¼ C.	Dried basil	
1 Tbsp.	Salt	
1 Tbsp.	Pepper	
½ C.	Dried porcini mushrooms	
½ C.	Fresh basil	Chopped

EQUIPMENT

Name of Equipment	Special Instructions/Notes
8-11 quart saucepan	
Sieve or fine mesh strainer	

DIRECTIONS

Step 1

Getting the tomatoes ready for sauce making- first, open the tomato can. Take one tomato out of the can, open it with your fingers, and let the seeds fall out, into the can. Place the cleaned tomato into a separate bowl. Use the same process for all the remaining tomatoes.

Step 2

When you've finished deseeding the tomatoes, transfer a handful of them onto a cutting board and dice. Place the diced tomatoes into another bowl. When all tomatoes are chopped, set the bowl aside. Set the can of tomato juice aside as well.

Step 3

In an 8-11 quart saucepan over medium heat, add the olive oil- it should cover the bottom of the pan. Add the onions and cook for 5 minutes.

Step 4

Next, stir in the garlic and cook until golden brown, about 3 minutes.

Step 5

To remove all seeds from the tomato juice, pour the can through a sieve or fine mesh strainer into the saucepan. Discard the seeds. Stir and bring to a simmer for 10 minutes.

Step 6

Stir in the chopped tomatoes and cook for 20 minutes. Then, add the tomato paste, dried basil, salt, and pepper, and cook for another 20 minutes.

Step 7

Put the dried porcini mushrooms in a microwavable bowl with 1 C. water. Microwave it on high for 1 minute, then let it cool. Chop up the porcini mushrooms, reserving the water. Put the mushrooms and the water into the sauce. Add the fresh basil and let everything simmer for 20 minutes, stirring occasionally. Taste for seasonings, serve and enjoy!

Buon appetito!

Bechamel Sauce

A classic European base used for soups and thick, creamy sauces. This Bechamel sauce is pretty similar to my Alfredo Sauce, only it is thicker due to the amount of flour. You want a rich and thick bechamel because when making lasagna, it will hold the layers together rather than result in a soupy, thin mess.

Menu Planning

Makes: 3 Cups

TIMELINE

Prep Time	5 minutes
Cook Time	+ 20 minutes
Total Time to Serving	25 minutes

INGREDIENTS

Measurement	Ingredient	Special Instructions/Notes
½ lb.	Butter	
½ C.	All-Purpose Flour	You may substitute with Almond flour for a gluten-free alternative
½ qt.	Half and half	
½ C.	Good quality parmesan or romano cheese	Grated
1 tsp.	Garlic salt	
1 tsp.	White pepper	

EQUIPMENT

Name of Equipment	Special Instructions/Notes
2 small saucepans	

DIRECTIONS

Step 1

In a small saucepan, gently melt ½ lb. butter. Sprinkle in ½ cup flour and whisk for 5 minutes. Heat ½ qt half and half in another saucepan until steaming. Add the warm half and half to the butter/flour mixture and whisk together. The mixture will thicken in about 4 minutes, and continue to whisk.

Step 2

Add the cheese, garlic salt, and white pepper. Stir constantly. Once it thickens, remove from heat.

Buon appetito!

Alfredo Sauce

Butter, cream, and parmesan come together for this heavenly, creamy sauce. At the restaurant we made the traditional Alfredo Sauce with egg yolks every single day. To me, this is the epitome of Italian comfort food. Toss it with thick fettuccine noodles, or serve it over broccoli, chicken, or salmon.

Before You Get Started

- While I recommend using an egg yolk in the sauce (especially if you like an extra bit of decadence), in this recipe I also gave the option of substituting the egg yolk with flour, for ease of cooking.

- Be careful not to overheat the sauce once you add the egg or it will scramble.

- This recipe makes enough for two servings, but you can easily double or triple the recipe if you're serving a crowd.

Menu Planning

Serves: 2 people

Serves Well With:
- Fettuccine (or any pasta of choice)
- Broccoli
- Chicken
- Salmon

TIMELINE

Prep Time		10 minutes
Cook Time	+	25 minutes
Total Time to Serving		35 minutes

INGREDIENTS

Measurement	Ingredient	Special Instructions/Notes
4 C.	Half and half	
¼ lb.	Butter	
1 Tbsp	All-purpose flour	You may substitute with Almond flour for a gluten-free alternative
1 C.	High quality parmesan cheese or pecorino romano	Grated
1 tsp.	Garlic salt	
1 tsp.	White pepper	
½ tsp	Whole Nutmeg (optional)	Freshly grated
1 C.	Heavy cream	
1	Egg yolk	
	Salt	To taste

EQUIPMENT

Name of Equipment	Special Instructions/Notes
Two medium saucepans	

DIRECTIONS

Step 1

First, place a saucepan over medium heat and add the half and half, stirring occasionally as it warms.

Step 2

In a second saucepan over medium heat, melt the butter, then sprinkle in the flour and whisk until incorporated. Continue to cook and whisk for 5 minutes. Add the warmed half and half, cheese, and garlic salt, and white pepper to the saucepan. Stir and cook until it starts to thicken, about 5 minutes. Add the freshly grated nutmeg (optional).

Step 3

If you're using an egg yolk- put the heavy cream into a 4 cup measuring cup or large bowl. Add one egg yolk and whisk together. Slowly pour in one cup of the warmed half and half to the heavy cream/yolk mixture to temper the yolk, stirring while adding. Pour everything from the bowl into the pan and continue to cook over low heat for 10 minutes. If you would like a thinner sauce, you can add a little more half and half. Serve and enjoy!

If you aren't using an egg yolk- add the heavy cream to the saucepan and cook over low heat for 5 minutes. If you would like a thinner sauce, you can add a little more half and half. Serve and enjoy!

Step 4

Taste the Alfredo, and add more cheese and salt to taste. The quality of the cheese will affect how salty it is.

Buon appetito!

Preparing the Eggplant

This is my method for slicing and frying eggplant when making dishes such as stuffed eggplant, and eggplant parmigiana.

Before You Get Started

- **See photos** for help on how to properly slice.

TIMELINE

Prep Time	20 minutes
Cook Time	10 minutes
Cooling Time	+ 20 minutes
Total Time to Serving	50 minutes

INGREDIENTS

Measurement	Ingredient	Special Instructions/Notes
1	Large eggplant	
1 C.	All-purpose flour	You can substitute Almond flour for a gluten-free alternative
3	Eggs	Lightly beaten
2 C.	Canola oil	For frying

EQUIPMENT

Name of Equipment	Special Instructions/Notes
2 shallow dishes or pie plates	
Large wok or Dutch oven	

DIRECTIONS

Step 1

Place a layer of paper towels onto a baking sheet, cutting board, or flat surface. Place the eggplant on its own cutting board. Use a vegetable peeler to peel off the purple skin. Then, cut off both ends where it begins to taper. Slice the eggplant lengthwise, into ½ inch thick slices. Lay the eggplant onto the lined baking sheet, and lightly salt. This will bring out any excess water. Top with another paper towel layer, and continue to layer the sliced eggplant, salt, and paper towels until all the eggplant is on the baking sheet. Let it sit and drain for 15 minutes.

Step 2

Next, prepare a shallow dish or pie plate with flour. Prepare a second shallow dish or pie plate with the lightly beaten eggs.

Step 3

Heat canola oil in a large wok or dutch oven over medium-high heat. Make sure you have at least 2 inches of oil in the pan to cook eggplant evenly.

Step 4

Once the oil is hot enough, take one slice of eggplant at a time, lightly dredge in the flour bowl, then dip into the egg wash. Slowly place the eggplant into the hot oil, taking care so the oil does not splash. Repeat with remaining pieces of eggplant, cooking in batches as to not overcrowd the pan.

Step 5

Fry the eggplant on both sides until golden brown, about 4-5 minutes per side. Lay the cooked pieces on fresh paper towels to let cool, about 20 minutes.

Buon appetito!

Ricotta Cheese Mixture

This mixture is used for a few different recipes in the cookbook, including several of the lasagna recipes and the stuffed eggplant. It makes enough for a a pan of 12 rolls of stuffed eggplant. When making the Vegetable Lasagna and the Old World Lasagna with Hearty Bolognese recipes, be sure to double this Ricotta Cheese Mixture recipe. You can make this a few days in advance, simply cover and store in the fridge.

Menu Planning

Makes: 16 ounces

TIMELINE

Prep Time	5 minutes
Cook Time	+ 0 minutes
Total Time to Serving	5 minutes

INGREDIENTS

Measurement	Ingredient	Special Instructions/Notes
15 oz	Whole-milk ricotta cheese	Buy a good quality container with a name brand - the taste is different
3 Tbsp.	Pecorino Romano Cheese	Grated
1	Egg	
1 tsp	Salt	
1 tsp	Pepper	
1 tsp.	Italian seasoning	

DIRECTIONS

Step 1

Put the ricotta cheese in a small-medium sized bowl. Add the pecorino romano, egg, salt, pepper, and Italian seasoning.

Step 2

Mix all ingredients together and set aside. Taste to check seasonings. It should be cheesy and smooth.

Buon appetito!

Soups

Pasta e' Fagoili

Literally translated as "Pasta and Bean," this soup brings me back to my childhood. My earliest memory of Pasta e' Fagoili was when I was 8 years old and on a vacation in Miami. My dad couldn't come, so my mom brought takeout soup home for him on the airplane. My second memory of this soup was going to NYC and staying at the Gorham Hotel, which was owned by my dad's former boss, Jack Davis. The Italian Restaurant attached to the hotel made the most heavenly version of this soup, and it became our first stop whenever we visited the city.

Before You Get Started

Make sure to start this recipe the day before so you can soak the beans overnight. If you'd like to speed up the process, you can use three 12oz cans of Great Northern or white beans- no soaking required, and it will bring the cook time down to 30 minutes.

Menu Planning

Serves: 4 people

Serves Well With:
• Great, crusty bread

Prep Time		Overnight (if using dry beans) or 30 minutes (if using canned beans)
Cook Time	+	3 hours (if using the dry beans) or 30 minutes (if using canned beans)
Total Time to Serving		**12 hours or 1 hour**

INGREDIENTS

Measurement	Ingredient	Special Instructions/Notes
½ lb.	Great Northern Beans (or 2 large cans of Great Northern / White Beans)	
1 C.	Uncooked tubettini pasta or mini shell pasta	
4	Bay leaves	
1	Ham Hock	This can usually be found in the grocery store near the bacon and sewet. If you can't find ham hock, you may omit it, since there is still bacon in the recipe.
1 Tbsp	Ham base (or if you can't find this, you can use chicken base)	
1	Large carrot	Finely chopped
2	Celery stalks	Finely chopped
1 tsp. + ¼ C.	Olive oil	
1	Medium yellow onion	Diced
¼ lb.	Bacon	Diced (dice the bacon while raw)
¼ C.	Fresh garlic	Chopped
2 Tbsp.	Italian seasoning	
2 Tbsp.	Dried basil	
2 Tbsp.	Fresh Parsley	Chopped

Name of Equipment	Special Instructions/Notes
Strainer	
2-quart pot	For cooking the pasta
8-10 quart pot	For the soup
8-inch saute pan	For sauteing

DIRECTIONS

Step 1

Rinse and pick over the beans to discard any stones or bad beans. After cleaning them, fill a large bowl with the beans and cover with water, adding 4 inches over the top. Soak them in the water overnight.

Step 2

The next morning, begin by cooking the tubitteri or mini shell pasta. Bring a 2-quart pot of water with a generous amount of salt, to a boil. Following the directions on the box or package, cook the pasta until it is al dente, then drain and set aside while you continue to make the soup. Add 1 tsp olive oil to the pasta to keep it from sticking together.

Step 3

Rinse the beans in a strainer then place them into an 8-10-quart pot. If you are using canned beans, drain and rinse them, then add them now. Fill the pot with 12 cups of water. Heat over medium-high until it reaches a rolling boil, then adjust the heat to medium. Add the bay leaves, ham hock, ham base, carrots, and celery to the pot.

Step 4

On another burner, heat an 8-inch saute pan with ¼ C. olive oil. Add the onion and bacon, and cook until the bacon is fully cooked but not crispy. Add the garlic, Italian seasoning, and dried basil to the pan.

Step 5

Stir and continue to cook until the bacon is slightly crispy. Pour the mixture into the soup pot and turn the heat down to low. Simmer and cook the soup for 1 ½-2 hours, stirring occasionally. When you think it is done, taste a bean, and if it is no longer hard, the soup is done.

Step 6

Discard the ham hock from the soup. Check the ham hock to see if there is meat on the bone, If there is, cut the ham off, dice it, and put it back into the soup. Not all ham hocks are meaty.

Step 7
Ladle soup into individual bowls and garnish with freshly chopped parsley.

Buon appetito!

Carrot Potato Soup

This is a recipe I came up with at the store. Using a vegetable base would create a great vegetarian soup. I think the combination of root vegetables, bay leaf, and touch of butter and cream create a perfect blend.

Menu Planning

Makes: 6 small cups or 3 large bowls

Serves Well With:
- Good, crusty bread

Prep Time		30 minutes
Cook Time	+	40 minutes
Total Time to Serving		**1 hour, 10 minutes**

INGREDIENTS

Measurement	Ingredient	Special Instructions/Notes
6 C.	Vegetable or chicken broth	
1 Tbsp	Vegetable or chicken soup base	
1	Bay Leaf	
3	Medium russet potatoes	Peeled and diced into large pieces
6	Large carrots	Peeled and diced into large pieces
1	Medium yellow onion	Cut into 4 pieces
1 C.	Heavy cream	
4 Tbsp. / ½ stick	Butter	

EQUIPMENT

Name of Equipment	Special Instructions/Notes
4-6 qt. saucepan or dutch oven	
Blender or food processor	

DIRECTIONS

Step 1

Set a saucepan or dutch oven over medium-high heat.

Step 2

Add the vegetable or chicken broth, soup base, bay leaf, potatoes, carrots, and onions. Cook for 30 minutes, stirring occasionally. When vegetables are fork tender, use a blender or food processor to puree. Depending on the size of the machine, you may choose to blend in batches, as the soup will be hot.

Step 3

Clean out the saucepan and return blended soup to the stove over low heat. Add the heavy cream and butter and simmer for 15 more minutes.

Buon appetito!

Italian Onion Soup

I love this creamy, comforting soup because it's both super quick to make and full of flavor. It gets its creaminess from an egg yolk and a dash of cream.

Menu Planning

Makes: 4 cups

Serves Well With:
• Good, crusty bread

TIMELINE

How long will this recipe take from preparation to serving?

Prep Time		15 minutes
Cook Time	+	20 minutes
Total Time to Serving		**35 minutes**

INGREDIENTS

Measurement	Ingredient	Special Instructions/Notes
½ C.	Heavy cream	
1	Egg Yolk	
4 C.	Chicken broth or vegetable broth	
1 tsp.	Chicken base or vegetable base	
¼ C.	Salted butter	
1	Large yellow onion	Sliced lengthwise into thin strips.
1 Tbsp	All-purpose flour	You may substitute almond flour for a gluten-free alternative
1 tsp.	Salt	
1 tsp.	Pepper	

EQUIPMENT

Name of Equipment	Special Instructions/Notes
Small saucepan	
12-inch saucepan with 2 ½ inch deep sides or 4 qt. Dutch oven	

DIRECTIONS

Step 1

Into a medium bowl, pour 2 Tbsp. heavy cream and one egg yolk. Stir together, then set aside for later use. Place a small saucepan on the stove and heat the chicken or vegetable broth. Add the chicken or vegetable base to the broth and stir to dissolve.

Step 2

In a 12-inch saucepan or dutch oven, melt the butter over medium-low heat. Add the onions and cook for 20 minutes, until the onions are translucent.

Step 3

Sprinkle the flour into the onions and whisk to incorporate. Cook for 5 minutes.

Step 4

Add the warm chicken broth mixture to the onion mixture. Stir until it thickens. Then add salt, pepper, and the remainder of heavy cream.

Step 5

Slowly pour 1 C. of the chicken broth mixture into the bowl with the cream and egg yolk. Whisk it while you slowly add the hot liquid to temper the egg. When the egg mixture has warmed, add it to the soup. Do not boil the soup or the eggs will scramble. Taste the soup and season with salt and pepper as needed.

Buon appetito!

Creamy Tomato Basil Soup

Isn't tomato soup just the ultimate comfort food? I love to eat it with garlic toast. Obviously, serving it with grilled cheese makes a classic pairing, or bake up a cheesy baguette for a fresh take! My dad would put day-old baguette into this soup and let it soak up the creamy broth. He used to call it 'Bread Soup'.

Menu Planning

Makes: 6 8oz Servings (Soup Cups) or 3 Bowls

Serves Well With:

- Grilled Cheese Sandwich
- Garlic Toast or cheesy baguette
- Side salad with Balsamic Vinaigrette (p.72) or Caesar Dressing (p.74)
- Garnish with some Garlicky Croutons (p.76)

TIMELINE

Prep Time		15 minutes
Cook Time	+	50 minutes
Total Time to Serving		**1 hours, 5 minutes**

INGREDIENTS

Measurement	Ingredient	Special Instructions/Notes
¼ C.	Good-quality olive oil	
1	Medium yellow onion	Diced
¼ C. (½ stick)	Butter	
4 Tbsp.	Fresh garlic	Chopped
3 Tbsp	Dried basil	
32 oz.	Canned crushed italian tomatoes	I purchase 2 16-ounce cans
2 C.	Vegetable or chicken broth	
6oz	Tomato paste	
1 Tbsp	Salt	
1 Tbsp	Pepper	
1 pint	Heavy cream	
1 C.	Fresh basil	Chopped

EQUIPMENT

Name of Equipment	Special Instructions/Notes
4-6 quart soup pot or dutch oven	

DIRECTIONS

Step 1

In a 4-6-quart soup pot or dutch oven over medium-high heat, pour in the olive oil. Once the oil has warmed, stir in the onion and let cook for 5 minutes. Next add the butter, garlic, and dried basil, cook for 5 minutes more. Add the crushed tomatoes, broth, tomato paste, salt, and pepper to the pot. Cook for 30 minutes over medium heat, stirring occasionally. The soup should deepen in color to a dark red when it's almost done.

Step 2

Add the heavy cream and fresh basil and cook for 10 minutes more. Taste the soup and add salt and pepper if needed.

Buon appetito!

Mushroom Alfredo Soup

If you're like me and adore mushrooms, this is the soup for you. Rich and hearty, this soup is made with mushrooms, chicken broth, tomato paste, and a little cream. I love to serve it with some good, crusty bread and a side salad for a full dinner.

Menu Planning

Serves: 4 people

Serves Well With:
- Crusty bread
- A side salad tossed with Balsamic Vinaigrette (p.72)

(p.72)

TIMELINE

Prep Time		20 minutes
Cook Time	+	50 minutes
Total Time to Serving		**1 hour, 10 minutes**

INGREDIENTS

Measurement	Ingredient	Special Instructions/Notes
½ lb.	Butter	
16 oz	White button mushrooms	Sliced
¼ C.	Flour	
1 Tbsp.	Tomato paste	
5 pieces	Dried porcini mushrooms	
32 oz.	Chicken broth or vegetable broth	
1 Tbsp.	Chicken base or vegetable base	
½ pint	Heavy cream	
1 tsp.	Salt	
1 tsp.	Pepper	

EQUIPMENT

Name of Equipment	Special Instructions/Notes
4-6 qt. stockpot or dutch oven	

DIRECTIONS

Step 1

Place a 4 or 6 qt. stockpot or dutch oven over medium heat and melt butter. Add the mushrooms and saute until they are light brown, about 5 minutes.

Step 2

Using a whisk, slowly sprinkle the flour into the pot. Continue to cook and whisk for 5 minutes.

Step 4

Add the tomato paste and cook for 5 minutes, or until it has dissolved into the mushrooms. While the tomato paste is cooking down, put the dried porcini mushrooms in a microwavable bowl with 1 C. water. Microwave it on high for 1 minute, then let it cool, about 5 minutes. Chop up the porcini mushrooms, reserving the water. Add the mushrooms and the water into the pot. Then add both the broth and base. Bring to a simmer for 20 minutes, stirring occasionally.

Step 5

Add heavy cream, salt, and pepper to the pot. Bring the soup up to at least 180 degrees and serve. You may also cool and refrigerate up to 5 days, or cool and then freeze.

Buon appetito!

Corn Chowder

This recipe is a great one for substituting, omitting, and adding your favorite meats, vegetables, and spices- even adding in leftovers from your fridge. One of my favorite proteins to add is shrimp, elevating it into a delicious shrimp and corn chowder.

Menu Planning

Makes: 6 8oz Servings (Soup Cups) or 3 Bowls

Serves Well With:
- Crusty Bread

TIMELINE

Prep Time		30 minutes
Cook Time	+	40 minutes
Total Time to Serving		**1 hour, 10 minutes**

INGREDIENTS

Measurement	Ingredient	Special Instructions/Notes
⅓ C.	Olive Oil	
¼ C.	Uncooked bacon	Diced
1	Medium yellow onion	Diced
2 Tbsp.	Fresh garlic	Chopped
1	Large Carrot	Peeled and diced
2	Stalks Celery	Dice
¼ lb. / 1 stick	Butter	
1 tsp.	Italian seasoning	
2	Bay leaves	
6 C.	Vegetable or chicken broth	
1 Tbsp.	Vegetable or chicken soup base	
2	Medium russet potatoes	Peeled and cut into large cubes, set aside in a large bowl filled with water to prevent browning. Drain water before adding potatoes to soup.
3 C.	Fresh or frozen corn	You can use a 10.8 oz frozen bag
¼ C.	Heavy Cream	
1 Tbsp.	All-purpose flour	You may substitute almond flour to make it gluten-free
¼ C.	Fresh Parsley	Chopped
1 tsp.	Salt	
1 tsp.	Pepper	

EQUIPMENT

Name of Equipment	Special Instructions/Notes
6 qt. saucepan	

DIRECTIONS

Step 1

Place a 6 qt. saucepan over medium heat and add the olive oil. Once the oil is warm, add the bacon and onions and cook for 5 minutes, or until they are soft. Then add the garlic and cook for 5 minutes. Next, toss in the carrots, celery, butter, italian seasoning, and bay leaves. Let it cook for 5 minutes more. Add the broth, soup base and potatoes, cook for 15 minutes. Finally, add the corn and cook for an additional 10 minutes.

Step 2

In a small bowl, whisk the cream and flour together. Let it sit for a few minutes, then whisk it again. It should be free of lumps.

Step 3

Add the cream mixture to the soup and simmer for 20 minutes, it will gradually thicken the broth.

Step 4

Ladle the soup into bowls and sprinkle freshly chopped parsley on top. Add salt and pepper to taste.

Buon appetito!

Note: if making shrimp chowder, you may add raw shrimp (medium shrimp, 41/50 per lb) when adding the cream mixture to gently cook the shrimp.

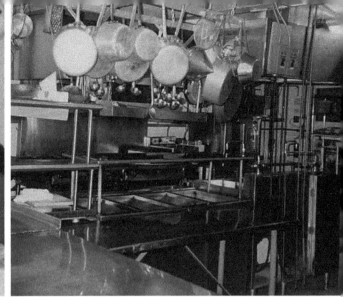

Villa Vespa

"a nice little
Italian Restaurant"

SPECIAL $11.95

Sides

GARLIC BREAD   50

SPINACH ALLA VILLA VESPA   53

HARICOTS VERTS WITH ROASTED
RED PEPPER AND GARLIC   56

Garlic Bread

At the restaurant we prepped a large quantity of our homemade garlic butter so we could quickly bake this garlic bread to-order. At the takeout store, it was probably our most popular item. One customer would come in every week in the summer and walk out with 8 or 9 baguettes. Truly the perfect side for every recipe in this book.

Before You Get Started

Look for a par-cooked bread in the freezer section or in specialty stores. The benefit is that it is almost like baking the bread on-spot. If you can't find par-cooked bread, look for a high quality baguette- crusty on the outside, soft in the middle.

Menu Planning

Makes: One baguette of garlic bread

TIMELINE

Prep Time		40 minutes
Cook Time	+	10 minutes
Total Time to Serving		**50 minutes**

INGREDIENTS

Measurement	Ingredient	Special Instructions/Notes
1 lb.	Salted butter	
¼ C.	Fresh garlic	Chopped
1 Tbsp.	Butcher or course ground pepper	
1 tsp.	Garlic salt	
1	Good quality, crusty baguette	

EQUIPMENT

Name of Equipment	Special Instructions/Notes
Baking sheet	

DIRECTIONS

Step 1

Preheat the oven to 325 degrees. Soften butter slightly, so it is mixable- room temperature is best.

Step 2

Cut the butter into cubes and place in a medium bowl. Add the garlic, pepper, and garlic salt. Mix until everything is incorporated.

Step 3

Cut a baguette in half lengthwise. Liberally spread the garlic butter on both halves. Place on a baking sheet and cook in the oven for 10 minutes.

Buon appetito!

Spinach Alla Villa Vespa

Sauteed spinach with mushrooms, garlic, and Villa Vespa Marinara Sauce. This versatile side dish was a super seller at the takeout store. It's great on its own, or delicious on a bed of pasta.

Menu Planning

Serves: 4 people

TIMELINE

Prep Time		20 minutes
Cook Time	+	20 minutes
Total Time to Serving		40 minutes

INGREDIENTS

Measurement	Ingredient	Special Instructions/Notes
4 C. / 16 oz	Fresh spinach	
¼ C.	Extra Virgin Olive Oil	
1 Tbsp.	Fresh garlic	Chopped
5	White button mushrooms	Sliced
4 Tbsp	Salted butter	
1 tsp	Salt	
1 tsp	Pepper	
1 C.	Villa Vespa Marinara Sauce	Recipe on page 13

EQUIPMENT

Name of Equipment	Special Instructions/Notes
9-inch wok or 12-inch saucepan	
Cheesecloth (optional)	
12-inch saute pan	

DIRECTIONS

Step 1

First, steam the spinach- place 4-inches of water in a 9-inch wok or 12-inch saucepan over high heat and add a pinch of salt. Bring to a boil, then add the spinach, a little at a time, allowing it to cook down. Cook for 4 minutes, then remove from the heat and drain the spinach. Squeeze all excess water from the spinach, using either a cheesecloth, paper towels, or just your hands. Return it to the saucepan or wok, with the burner off. Stir in salt and pepper, then place a lid on it to keep warm.

Step 2

Set a 12-inch saute pan over medium heat and add olive oil. Once the oil has warmed slightly, add the garlic and mushrooms and cook for 4 minutes. Transfer the spinach to the saute pan and stir all the ingredients together.

Step 3

Stir in the butter, salt, and pepper. Then add the marinara sauce. Continue to heat and stir until the mixture is warm, then serve.

Buon appetito!

Haricots Verts with Roasted Red Peppers and Garlic

This french green bean is slightly longer and thinner than the standard string bean. You can usually find them in either the fresh produce or the freezer section of the grocery store. One thing I love about this recipe is the fact that it's a one pan dish. Enjoy it as a side or toss it in some cooked pasta to make it a main course. Dinner done!

Menu Planning

Serves: 4-6 people

Serves Well With:
- Pasta of Choice (I like to use Spaghetti)
- Chicken Parmesan (p.103)
- Any Main Course

TIMELINE

Prep Time		15 minutes
Cook Time	+	10 minutes
Total Time to Serving		**45 minutes**

INGREDIENTS

Measurement	Ingredient	Special Instructions/Notes
1 lb. bag	Fresh or frozen haricots verts	
3 Tbsp.	Extra virgin olive oil	
1	Small yellow bell pepper	Cut lengthwise into strips
1	Small red bell pepper	Cut lengthwise into strips
1 Tbsp.	Fresh garlic	Chopped
	Salt	
	Pepper	

EQUIPMENT

Name of Equipment	Special Instructions/Notes
Medium-sized wok or saucepan	Must fit at least 6 cups
Medium Strainer	

DIRECTIONS

Step 1

In a medium wok or saucepan, add 2 cups of water and 1 tsp. salt. Bring to a boil. Add all the green beans and ensure they are fully covered in the water. Simmer for 5 minutes.

Step 2

Once the green beans have cooked, pour them into a strainer and set aside. Pour and wipe out all the water from the wok and add the olive oil to the pan over medium heat. Add sliced peppers to the pan and cook 5-7 minutes, stirring often so that they do not burn.

Step 3

Next add the garlic and stir, cooking 3-4 minutes, or until golden brown. Add the green beans back in and stir again. Finish with salt and pepper to taste.

Buon appetito!

Appetizers

Clams Italian

This big, beautiful bowl of steamed littleneck clams cooked in marinara sauce and white wine was a popular appetizer at the Villa Vespa restaurant. Garlic bread is a must to soak up all the wonderful sauce.

Menu Planning

Serves: 2 people

Serves Well With:
- Garlic Bread (p.50)

Garlic Bread (p.50)

TIMELINE

Prep Time		10 minutes
Cook Time	+	15 minutes
Total Time to Serving		25 minutes

INGREDIENTS

Measurement	Ingredient	Special Instructions/Notes
20	Littleneck clams	
2 Tbsp	Olive Oil	
1 Tbsp	Fresh garlic	Chopped
½ tsp	Crushed red pepper (optional)	
3 C.	Villa Vespa Marinara Sauce	Recipe on page 13
¼ C.	White wine or vegetable broth	
¼ C.	Fresh basil	Finely cshopped or julienned

EQUIPMENT

Name of Equipment	Special Instructions/Notes
Slotted spoon or fine mesh sieve	For cleaning the clams, if you don't have either, you may remove with your hands
11-12-inch saucepan or wok with a lid	

DIRECTIONS

Step 1

First clean the clams. In a large bowl of cold water, add a dash of salt, then add the clams and allow to soak, about 5 minutes. Scoop them out with a slotted spoon or fine mesh sieve, don't pour them out to drain them or any expelled sand will fall back onto them. Discard any clams that are not fully closed.

Step 2

Warm the olive oil in a saucepan or wok over medium heat. Add the garlic and crushed red pepper (optional), cook for 4 minutes. Then add the marinara sauce, clams, and white wine or vegetable broth. Stir and cover with a lid. Cook for 10-15 minutes, until all clams have opened.

Step 3

When clams are cooked, sprinkle in fresh basil, stir, and serve.

Buon appetito!

Chicken Liver Pate

This recipe is a personal favorite of mine. One summer at the restaurant, my dad hired an Italian chef who was retiring and had plans to move back to Italy. He was previously a chef at The White House during President Carter's administration. This was his recipe. I must admit, he did not give it to me. I was around 16 or 17 at the time and would just watch him cook, learning the recipe through observing.

Menu Planning

Makes: 3 Cups

Serves Well With:
* Crackers or good, hard bread
* Fresh or dried fruit

Prep Time		30 minutes
Cook Time		40 minutes
Cool Time	+	30 minutes
Total Time to Serving		**1 hour, 40 minutes**

INGREDIENTS

Measurement	Ingredient	Special Instructions/Notes
2 Tbsp.	Extra Virgin Olive Oil	
½ lb.	Raw bacon	Diced
½	Medium yellow onion	Diced
8 oz	Container of fresh chicken livers	Cleaned of fatty tissue and halved
1 Tbsp	Fresh garlic	Chopped
1 C.	Brandy	Use high quality
2	Hard boiled eggs	Roughly chopped
1 tsp.	Salt	
1 tsp.	Pepper	

EQUIPMENT

Name of Equipment	Special Instructions/Notes
12-inch saucepan with a lid	
Food processor (or you may chop by hand)	

DIRECTIONS

Step 1

In a 12-inch saucepan over medium heat, pour in the olive oil. Add the diced bacon and onions, cook for 10 minutes, stirring occasionally.

Step 2

Next add in the cleaned chicken livers and garlic, cook 15 minutes, continuing to stir.

Step 3

When the livers are cooked through and the bacon is crisp, add the hardboiled eggs and the brandy. If you prefer to cook out the alcohol, after adding it to the pan, light it with a match. Stand back as it will flame up. Let it burn for 3 minutes then put out the flame with a metal lid. Stir everything to combine. Remove from heat and let cool completely, about 30 minutes.

Step 4

When the mixture has cooled to room temperature, transfer it to a food processor and pulse until smooth. You can also chop it by hand until smooth and creamy.

Buon appetito!

Fried Calamari with Spicy Marinara Sauce

This calamari recipe is SO good. I'm often disappointed when I order calamari out at a restaurant, because this dish is exactly what I'm expecting and craving. I think there are two factors that set it apart- first, the mixture itself is just perfect. Second, the frying method of using a high temperature oil to produce a "flash fry" is crucial. We flash fry so the outside of the calamari immediately sears. It does not become saturated in oil nor does it overcook (which would render it chewy). The resulting dish is an almost light and tender fried appetizer. And the cherry on top? It is SO good dunked in the Villa Vespa Marinara Sauce, or with a sprinkle of salt and a squeeze of fresh lemon juice.

Before You Get Started

The quantity of squid in this recipe does not really matter. Feel free to cook more if you'd like.

Menu Planning

Serves: Appetizers for 4 people

TIMELINE

Prep Time		15 minutes
Cook Time	+	30 minutes
Total Time to Serving		**45 minutes**

INGREDIENTS

Measurement	Ingredient	Special Instructions/Notes
1 Tbsp.	Olive oil	
1 tsp.	Fresh garlic	Chopped
1 tsp.	Crushed red pepper (optional)	
2 C.	Villa Vespa Marinara Sauce	Recipe on page 13
4 C.	Canola Oil	For frying
1 C.	All-purpose flour	
¼ C.	"Complete" Pancake Mix	"Complete" meaning any pancake mix where you only need add water
32 oz.	Frozen squid bodies with tentacles or fresh squid that's been cleaned and cut by your local fishmonger	Dry squid bodies with paper towels and slice into 1-inch circular pieces
1 Tbsp.	Salt	
1	Lemon	Cut into wedges for serving

EQUIPMENT

Name of Equipment	Special Instructions/Notes
6-inch saute pan with lid	
Baking sheet	
12-inch wok or 6 qt. Dutch oven	For frying
Small mesh sieve or strainer	
Metal slotted spoon	

DIRECTIONS

Step 1

Place a 6-inch saute pan on the stove and add the olive oil over medium-low heat. Once the oil is warm, add the garlic and crushed red pepper. If you aren't a fan of spice, you may omit the crushed red pepper. Cook for 3 minutes, until the garlic is golden brown. Then add the marinara sauce and increase the heat to medium, cooking for 5 minutes. Remove from heat and cover with a lid to keep warm while you make the calamari.

Step 2

Line a baking sheet with paper towels. In a wok or dutch oven add the canola oil and heat between medium-high and high heat- the oil should reach 375 degrees before frying.

Step 3

While the oil is coming up to temperature, combine the flour and pancake mix in a bowl. Stir to mix completely.

Step 4

Drop ⅓ of the squid into the flour bowl to dredge. Mix well, then scoop it out using a small mesh sieve or strainer and shake overtop the bowl to shake off any excess flour.

Step 5

Carefully, drop the squid into the hot oil. Fry for 2-3 minutes- it will be golden brown. Remove the squid with a slotted spoon and place on the paper towel lined baking sheet. While it is still hot, sprinkle it with salt.

Step 6

Continue to fry the squid in batches, salting each batch after placing the squid onto the towel lined baking sheet. Once all the squid has been cooked, turn off the heat and let the fryer oil sit until it has completely cooled.

Step 7

Place the calamari on a serving platter with a bowl of the spicy marinara sauce and some lemon wedges.

Buon appetito!

Salad Dressings

Balsamic Vinaigrette

I came up with this recipe during my time as a private chef, in between the restaurant's closing and the opening of my takeout store. In my opinion, store-bought dressings don't hold a candle to homemade ones. The taste is fresher, it's cheaper, and you can control the quality of the ingredients, so it isn't full of additives.

Menu Planning

Makes: 16 ounces

Prep Time	15 minutes
Total Time to Serving	20 minutes

INGREDIENTS

Measurement	Ingredient	Special Instructions/Notes
3 Tbsp.	Dijon mustard	
½ C.	Balsamic Vinegar	
½	White Vinegar	
4 Tbsp.	Aged balsamic Vinegar or Balsamic Glaze	
1 C.	Good quality olive oil	
¾ C.	Water	
3 Tbsp.	Sugar	
	Salt	
	Pepper	

EQUIPMENT

Name of Equipment	Special Instructions/Notes
Food processor or blender	

DIRECTIONS

Step 1

In a food processor or blender, add the mustard, balsamic vinegar, white vinegar, and aged balsamic or balsamic glaze. Turn it on and, with the motor running, slowly add the olive oil through the top of the machine.

Step 2

Once all the oil has been incorporated, stop the motor. Begin to pulse, slowly adding the water. Check the consistency at this point to get the thickness that you desire. You may not need all of the water. Add the sugar and pulse to mix, being careful not to overmix or the dressing will break. Adding more oil will also cause the dressing to break.

Step 3

Taste the dressing and add salt and pepper to taste. The dressing may be covered and kept in the refrigerator for up to 4 weeks.

Buon appetito!

Caesar Dressing

This is the best caesar dressing I've ever had. No lie. A young woman who worked in the kitchen at The Villa taught me the recipe. She was a graduate of The Baltimore International College in Culinary Arts and found her way to Lake Placid for a season. Come to think of it, I actually learned a lot from her.

Before You Get Started

Don't skip the anchovy paste- this not only gives it a nice saltiness, it's what makes it a Caesar. You'll find the paste in the condiment aisle of the grocery store.

Menu Planning

Makes: 16 ounces

TIMELINE

Prep Time	15 minutes
Total Time to Serving	15 minutes

INGREDIENTS

Measurement	Ingredient	Special Instructions/Notes
3	Egg yolks	
½ C.	Parmesan cheese	Grated
1 Tbsp.	Fresh garlic	Chopped
1 tsp.	Salt	
1 tsp.	Pepper	
½	Lemon	Juiced (should make ¼ C. juice)
1 Tbsp.	Dijon mustard	(no substitute)
1 tsp.	Anchovy paste or crushed anchovies	
2 C.	Canola Oil	
½ C.	Water	

EQUIPMENT

Name of Equipment	Special Instructions/Notes
Food processor or blender	

DIRECTIONS

Step 1

Add three egg yolks, parmesan, garlic, salt, pepper, lemon juice, dijon mustard, and anchovy paste to your food processor or blender. Pulse for 2 minutes to combine.

Step 2

Turn it on to low speed and with the motor running, slowly pour in all the canola oil. Continue to blend for 4 minutes. This will make the dressing thick and creamy, almost like a mayonnaise. Continue to blend and slowly pour in the water to loosen the consistency slightly. Taste and add more salt, pepper, or lemon juice as desired.

Buon appetito!

Garlicky Croutons

You will never eat premade croutons again.

Once the croutons are in the oven, keep a close eye on them as they will burn quickly.

Menu Planning

Makes: Enough for 4 salads

Prep Time		15 minutes
Cook Time		15-20 minutes
Cool Time	+	20 minutes
Total Time to Serving		**50-55 minutes**

INGREDIENTS

Measurement	Ingredient	Special Instructions/Notes
½	French baguette	Diced into 1-inch cubes
½ C.	Olive oil	
1 tsp.	Salt	
1 tsp.	Pepper	
1 Tbsp.	Fresh Garlic	Chopped
1 Tbsp.	Italian seasoning	

EQUIPMENT

Name of Equipment	Special Instructions/Notes
Baking sheet	
Metal spatula	

DIRECTIONS

Step 1

Preheat the oven to 350 degrees. Place the bread cubes in a bowl. Add the olive oil, salt, pepper, garlic, and italian seasoning and toss to coat.

Step 2

Lay the seasoned bread cubes on a baking sheet and place in the oven for 10 minutes, until they are golden brown. Remove from the oven and stir the croutons with a spatula to turn them over. Place them back in the oven and bake for an additional 10 minutes. Don't walk away as they will burn quickly.

Step 3

Take the croutons out of the oven and let cool. To save them for later, put them in a ziploc bag or airtight container and store for up to 4 days.

Buon appetito!

Vegetarian Entrees

Spaghetti with Garlic and Oil

This may be one of the simplest dishes in this book, and yet, it is so perfect. In fact, this would be a wonderful recipe to share with someone who is just learning to cook. Rather than overcomplicating it with too many ingredients, this dish is a celebration of the Italian staples - namely, pasta, garlic, and olive oil. Do not underestimate the flavors that good quality olive oil and garlic provide here.

Menu Planning

Serves: 2 people

Serves Well With:

- Caesar Salad (Dressing on p.74)
- Garden Salad with Balsamic dressing (Dressing on p.72)

(Dressing on p.74) (Dressing on p.72)

TIMELINE

Prep Time	15 minutes
Cook Time	+ 15 minutes
Total Time to Serving	30 minutes

INGREDIENTS

Measurement	Ingredient	Special Instructions/Notes
¼ lb.	Spaghetti (or your favorite pasta)	
1 Tbsp + ⅔ C.	Extra Virgin Olive Oil	
⅓ C.	Fresh garlic	Chopped
1 Tbsp.	Pepper	Preferably "Butcher ground", course, or freshly ground pepper
½ tsp.	Red pepper flakes or crushed red pepper (optional, if you like it spicy)	
1 Tbsp.	Butter	
⅓ C.	Fresh parsley	Chopped
1 tsp.	Sea Salt	

EQUIPMENT

Name of Equipment	Special Instructions/Notes
4-6-quart saucepan or stockpot	For cooking the pasta
Strainer or colander	
9-inch saute pan or wok	

DIRECTIONS

Step 1

Place a large stockpot on the stove and add enough water to cover your pasta. Add a generous amount of salt and bring the water to a boil. Cook the pasta according to the directions on the box or package. When it's done cooking, drain it into a strainer or colander. Add 1 Tbsp olive oil and toss to prevent it from sticking together.

Step 2

Place a 9-inch saute pan or wok over medium heat and add ⅔ C. olive oil. Add the garlic, pepper, and red pepper flakes (if you like it a little spicy). Cook 3-4 minutes, stirring, until the garlic is golden. Make sure to watch to ensure the garlic doesn't burn.

Step 3

Add the butter and cooked pasta to the pan. Toss the pasta to mix everything together.

Step 4

Top with chopped parsley and salt. Toss again. Plate and serve!

Buon appetito!

Pasta Primavera

This is actually an American dish that originated in the 1970s, typically consisting of pasta and fresh vegetables. We made our version a little more decadent. In this recipe we top a creamy, homemade fettuccine alfredo with cooked broccoli, cauliflower, green beans, sweet bell peppers, onion, and zucchini, with lots of fresh basil. You may add or omit any veggies of your choosing. I love the combination of the fresh vegetables with the creamy Alfredo Sauce.

Before You Get Started

- Because there is a decent amount of preparation that goes into chopping the veggies, I suggest making the Alfredo Sauce (p.21) ahead of time. If you haven't made a homemade Alfredo Sauce before, I can't recommend it enough. It's the simplest of all the sauces in this book, and take my word for it, store-bought sauce really just can't compare.

- Another way to streamline the dish is to put each vegetable into its own bowl after peeling, slicing, and prepping.

Menu Planning

Serves: 4 people

TIMELINE

Prep Time		50 minutes
Cook Time	+	30 minutes
Total Time to Serving		**2 hours, 15 minutes**

INGREDIENTS

Measurement	Ingredient	Special Instructions/Notes
1 Tbsp + 1 tsp	Salt	
1 C.	Fresh cauliflower	Cut into small 2-inch pieces
3 C.	Fresh broccoli	Cut into small 2-inch pieces
2 C.	Haricots verts or Green beans	Fresh or frozen
1	Small zucchini and/or yellow squash	Zucchini peeled in stripes and sliced into rounds; or Squash cut into 1-inch cubes
1 lb.	Fettuccine nests of imported Italian pasta or quality fettuccine (ideally Italian)	I recommend using the brands Colavita or De Cecco
4 C.	Homemade Alfredo Sauce	Recipe on page 21
½ C.	Olive oil	
1	Medium yellow onion	Sliced
1	Yellow bell pepper	Sliced into thin strips
1 Tbsp.	Fresh garlic	Chopped
½ C.	Fresh basil	Chopped
	Salt	To taste
	Pepper	To taste

EQUIPMENT

Name of Equipment	Special Instructions/Notes
8-quart saucepan	To cook the pasta
12-inch saucepan with lid or 10-inch wok with lid	To steam the vegetables
Strainer	
10-inch saute pan	To cook the Alfredo Sauce and toss the pasta

DIRECTIONS

Step 1

Have all your vegetables cut and placed in their own separate bowls. Begin to heat the water for the pasta, adding a generous amount of salt to the stockpot.

Step 2

In a large saucepan or wok, add 3 cups of water and 1 Tbsp. salt and bring to a boil. Once the water is boiling, add the cauliflower and cook for 5 minutes. Next, add the broccoli and haricots verts or green beans, cook for another 5 minutes. Then add the zucchini and/or yellow squash. Top the pan with a lid and steam the veggies, 3-4 minutes.

Step 3

Remove the lid and pour into a strainer to drain all the steamed vegetables. Leave them in the strainer, do not rinse with water.

Step 4

Cook the pasta according to the directions on the box or package. While the pasta is cooking, heat a 10-inch saute pan on low and add Alfredo Sauce to the pan.

Step 4

Dry the saucepan or wok you cooked the vegetables in, and return it to the stove. Add olive oil to the pan and set over medium-high heat. Add the onions and peppers, cook for 5 minutes. Then add the garlic and cook 5 minutes more, stirring everything to incorporate. Add the vegetables from the strainer and stir everything together. Sprinkle in 1 tsp salt, pepper, and all the fresh basil. Turn off the heat and set the pan off to the side.

Step 5

Drain the cooked fettuccine noodles and put them in the saute pan with the Alfredo Sauce. Toss to coat, and warm over medium-high heat. Serve the pasta and Alfredo Sauce on individual plates or a large serving platter. Lay the vegetables on top and season with salt and pepper. Enjoy!

Buon appetito!

Penne all'Arrabbiata

Penne pasta with spicy marinara sauce and peas. This was one of my dad's favorites. Penne all'Arrabbiata is found in many Italian restaurants. Arrabbiata means angry in Italian, so this dish is supposed to be spicy!

Menu Planning

Serves: 2-3 people

Serves Well With:
- Spinach Alla Villa Vespa (p.53)
- Haricots Verts with Roasted Red Peppers and Garlic (p.56)
- Side salad made with Balsamic Vinaigrette (p.72) or Caesar Dressing (p.74)

TIMELINE

Prep Time		10 minutes (does not include the time to make the Villa Vespa marinara sauce)
Cook Time	+	20 minutes
Total Time to Serving		**30 minutes**

INGREDIENTS

Measurement	Ingredient	Special Instructions/Notes
½ lb.	Penne Rigate pasta	
3 Tbsp.	Extra Virgin olive oil	
¼ C.	Fresh garlic	Chopped
1 Tbsp.	Crushed red pepper	
3 C.	Villa Vespa Marinara Sauce	Recipe on page 13
1 C.	Frozen peas	
¼ C.	Fresh basil	Chopped
1 Tbsp.	Salt	
1 Tbsp.	Course ground pepper	

EQUIPMENT

Name of Equipment	Special Instructions/Notes
6-8 quart stockpot	
Sieve or colander	
12-inch saute pan or wok	

Step 1

Put a 6-8 quart stock pot on the stove. Fill the pot halfway with water, add a generous amount of salt, and bring to a boil. When the water is heating up, begin making the sauce.

Step 2

Place a 12-inch saute pan or wok on a burner over medium heat. Pour olive oil into the pan. When the oil is warm, add the garlic and cook until golden brown, 2 minutes.

Step 3

Add the crushed red pepper, all the marinara sauce, fresh basil, salt, and pepper. Increase the heat to medium-high and simmer for 10 minutes, stirring occasionally. While the sauce is simmering, cook the pasta.

Step 3

Add the penne rigate to the boiling water and cook according to the directions on the box or package. Once the pasta is done cooking, drain it into a sieve or colander and stir 1 Tbsp olive oil into pasta to prevent the noodles from sticking together.

Step 4

Add the pasta to the sauce and mix well. Add the frozen peas and cook for 5 minutes more.

Buon appetito!

Eggplant Parmigiana

In my version of classic eggplant parmiginia, where thinly sliced eggplant gets deep-fried and baked with marinara sauce, mozzarella, and parmesan, I omit the breadcrumbs. Doing without allows one to truly taste the eggplant. It can easily be transformed into a gluten-free dish by substituting all-purpose flour for almond flour.

As written, the recipe is for 2 people- and can be easily doubled or tripled. If you are increasing the quantities, keep in mind that you will need a larger baking dish (or even multiple dishes) to accommodate.

Menu Planning

Serves: 2 people

Serves Well With:
- Pasta of Choice on side
- Spinach alla Villa Vespa (p.53)
- Green Beans Recipe (p.56)

TIMELINE

Prep Time		30 minutes (not including time to make Villa Vespa Marinara Sauce)
Cook Time	+	40 minutes
Total Time to Serving		**1 hours**

INGREDIENTS

Measurement	Ingredient	Special Instructions/Notes
1	Large eggplant	Sliced, dredged in flour, battered in egg wash, and deep-fried; For directions, see "Prepping the Eggplant" on page 23
1 C.	All-purpose four	You can substitute Almond flour for a gluten-free alternative
6	Eggs	Lightly beaten
3 C.	Vegetable or Canola oil	For frying the eggplant
4 C.	Villa Vespa Marinara Sauce	Recipe on page 13
3 C.	Shredded mozzarella cheese	
1 C.	Grated parmesan cheese	
1 tsp.	Salt	
1 tsp.	Pepper	
1 tsp.	Italian Seasoning	

EQUIPMENT

Name of Equipment	Special Instructions/Notes
11-inch wok or 12-inch saute pan	For frying the eggplant
8x5x2 inch bread/casserole pan	Glass or metal

DIRECTIONS

Step 1

Preheat the oven to 350 degrees. Prep, fry, and cool the eggplant (see "Prepping the Eggplant" on page 23). Put 1 C. of the marinara sauce on the bottom of the bread/casserole pan.

Step 2

Lay 2 pieces of eggplant on top of the marinara, covering the entire bottom of the pan.

Step 3

Add 1 C. mozzarella and ⅓ C. parmesan. Sprinkle the Italian seasoning on top.

Step 4

Add another layer of eggplant, 2 pieces, then top with another 1 ½ C. marinara sauce. Sprinkle another 1 C. shredded mozzarella and ⅓ C. grated parmesan on top.

Step 5

Add a final layer of eggplant, the last 2 pieces, top with 1 ½ C. marinara sauce, and finish with the remaining cheese.

Step 5

Place in the oven and bake for 35 minutes. It should be golden brown, hot, and bubbling.

Buon appetito!

Stuffed Eggplant

In this classic Italian dish, thinly sliced and fried eggplant is filled with ricotta cheese, then rolled in a bed of marinara sauce and baked with mozzarella and parmesan.

Before You Get Started

Before starting the recipe below, there are ingredients and instructions on how to properly cut and fry the eggplant under "Prepping the Eggplant," p.23. Similarly, make the Ricotta Cheese Mixture by following the ingredients and instructions under "Ricotta Cheese Mixture," p.25.

Menu Planning

Serves: 2 people

Serves Well With:
- A nice salad made with Balsamic Vinaigrette (p.72) or Caesar Dressing (p.74)
- Garlic Bread (p.50)

TIMELINE

Prep Time		30 minutes
Cook Time	+	40 minutes
Total Time to Serving		**1 hour**

INGREDIENTS

Measurement	Ingredient	Special Instructions/Notes
1	Large, firm eggplant	Sliced and fried- see "Prepping the Eggplant" for ingredients and directions on page 23
16 ounces	Ricotta Cheese Mixture	See "Ricotta Cheese Mixture" for ingredients and directions on page 25
2 C.	Villa Vespa Marinara Sauce	Recipe on page 13
½ tsp.	Italian Seasoning	
1 tsp.	Salt	
1 tsp.	Pepper	
1 C.	Mozzarella Cheese	Shredded
½ C.	Good quality Parmesan Cheese	Grated

EQUIPMENT

Name of Equipment	Special Instructions/Notes
8x8 Casserole pan or 9-inch pie plate	

DIRECTIONS

Step 1

Preheat the oven to 350 degrees. Prepare the eggplant by following the directions under "Prepping the Eggplant," page 23. Prepare the "Ricotta Cheese Mixture" by following instruction on page 25.

Step 2

Lay a thin layer of marinara sauce on the bottom of the casserole pan or pie plate, about 1 C.

Step 3

Dollop 2 Tbsp of the ricotta mixture into the middle of each piece of eggplant. Take the end of the eggplant and roll it over the dollop of ricotta and keep rolling to the other side.

Step 4

Place each rolled eggplant into the pan with marinara, with loose end down so it does not un-roll. Once all eggplant rolls have been placed in the pan, add a line of marinara atop each roll and sprinkle with Italian seasoning, salt, and pepper. Top with shredded mozzarella and parmesan cheese. Bake for 25 minutes.

Buon appetito!

Vegetable Lasagna

For those who love to be meatless, but don't want to compromise on flavor, this recipe is a huge hit.

Before You Get Started

This is an advanced recipe with a lot of prep work and several steps- you can make the Bechamel sauce (p.20), the Villa Vespa Marinara sauce (p.13), and the Ricotta Cheese Mixture (p.25) in advance to speed up the process.

Menu Planning

Serves: 6-8 people

Prep Time	40 minutes (Does not include time to make bechamel or Villa Vespa marinara sauces)
Cook Time	+ 40 minutes
Total Time to Serving	**1 hour, 20 minutes**

INGREDIENTS

Measurement	Ingredient	Special Instructions/Notes
3 C.	Bechamel Sauce	Recipe on page 20
4 C.	Villa Vespa Marinara sauce	Recipe on page 13
32 ounces	Ricotta Cheese Mixture	Recipe on page 25, double the recipe for the right quantity
4 C.	Fresh spinach	
⅓ C.	Olive oil	
1	Small onion	Diced
1	Sweet red bell pepper	Seeded and diced
1	Small zucchini	Peeled and diced
1 Tbsp.	Fresh Garlic	Chopped
1 tsp.	Salt	
1 tsp.	Pepper	
	Oil Spray or butter	To grease the casserole pan, for spray I use Pam™
18 oz.	Oven-ready lasagna noodles	I purchase 2 9-ounce boxes
4 C.	Shredded mozzarella cheese	
3 C.	Romano or Pamesan cheese	

EQUIPMENT

Name of Equipment	Special Instructions/Notes
Cheesecloth (optional)	
8 x 10 x 3 inch casserole pan	
Medium saute pan	

DIRECTIONS

Step 1

First, prepare the bechamel sauce (see "Bechamel sauce" recipe on page 20), Villa Vespa marinara sauce (see "Villa Vespa Marinara Sauce on page 13), and the Ricotta Cheese Mixture (see "Ricotta Cheese Mixture" on page 25). Set them aside until ready to assemble lasagna.

Step 2

Preheat the oven to 350 degrees.

Step 3

Steam the spinach- place 4-inches of water in a 9-inch wok or 12-inch saucepan over high heat and add a pinch of salt. Bring to a boil, then add the spinach, a little at a time, allowing it to cook down. Cook for 4 minutes, then remove from the heat and drain the spinach. Squeeze all excess water from the spinach, using either a cheesecloth, paper towels, or just your hands. Return it to the saucepan or wok, with the burner off. Stir in salt and pepper, then place a lid on it to keep warm.

Step 3

In a 10-12-inch saute pan, add the olive oil over medium heat. To the same pan add onions, red bell pepper, and zucchini, stir and cook for 5 minutes. Add the garlic and cook for 5 minutes more. Add the cooked spinach, salt, and pepper. Stir all ingredients together, then take off the heat and set aside.

Step 4

To assemble the lasagna, first grease the bottom of a casserole pan with oil spray or butter. Add a layer of the marinara sauce, about 2 C. Add a layer of pasta. Add 2 C. shredded mozzarella. Add another layer of pasta. Add all of the Ricotta Cheese Mixture, and spread evenly. Add a double layer of pasta. Add the entire vegetable mixture. Pour the bechamel sauce on top and spread evenly. Add another layer of pasta. Add 2 C. marinara sauce. Finish with 2 C. shredded mozzarella and pecorino or parmesan on top.

Step 5

Bake in the oven for 40 minutes.

Buon appetito!

Risotto Milanese

This risotto is a great accompaniment to many of the dishes in this book. My two favorite ways to serve it are either topped with Shrimp Marinara (p.171) or Bolognese Sauce (p.16).

Before You Get Started

See the notes below the recipe on optional varieties on the dish-including the addition of dried porcini mushrooms, fresh mushrooms, and parmesan cheese.

Menu Planning

Serves: 6 people

Serves Well With:
- Shrimp Marinara (p.171)
- Bolognese Sauce on top (p.16)
- Haricots Verts w/ Roasted Peppers and Garlic (p.56)
- Topped with mixed vegetables to make a risotto primavera

TIMELINE

Prep Time	10 minutes
Cook Time	+ 45 minutes
Total Time to Serving	55 minutes

INGREDIENTS

Measurement	Ingredient	Special Instructions/Notes
8 C.	Chicken broth or vegetable broth	Use vegetable broth if you'd like to keep it vegetarian
1 Tbsp.	Chicken base or vegetable base	Use vegetable base if you'd like to keep it vegetarian
¼ lb.	Butter	
1	Medium yellow onion	Diced
1 tsp.	Salt	
1 tsp.	White pepper	
1 lb.	Italian arborio rice	
½ C.	Dry vermouth	
¼ tsp.	Saffron	

EQUIPMENT

Name of Equipment	Special Instructions/Notes
Medium saucepan	Big enough to hold 2 qt. chicken broth
8-quart saucepan or dutch oven	
Wooden spoon	
Ladle	

DIRECTIONS
Step 1

In a small saucepan, warm the chicken or vegetable broth and stir in the chicken or vegetable base to dissolve.

Step 2

Place an 8-quart saucepan or dutch oven over medium-high heat. Melt the butter and add the onions, salt, and white pepper. Using a wooden spoon, stir for 5 minutes.

Step 3

Add the rice to the butter and cook for 5 minutes, stirring constantly. Stir in the dry vermouth and saffron. Cook for another 3 minutes.

Step 4

Slowly begin ladling the hot chicken broth to the rice mixture, one ladle at a time, continuing to stir the rice. Wait for the rice to absorb the broth before adding another ladle. Continue to slowly add the broth in this way, it should take about 40 minutes. If you run out of broth before the rice is fully cooked, simply heat a little more. Taste the rice to make sure it has the right doneness (or "toothiness"). It should be smooth and creamy, with a little bite to it. Add salt and pepper if necessary. Please taste it first so as to not oversalt it.

*Optional Variation 1: Adding Dried Porcini Mushrooms- you can add dried porcini mushrooms while cooking the rice. Rehydrate ¼ C. dry mushrooms (or a small handful) with ½ C. water to soak. Microwave for 30 seconds, then let them sit for 5 minutes. Chop the mushrooms and add them to the rice along with the water.

**Optional Variation 2: Adding Fresh Mushrooms- add fresh, sliced mushrooms, still raw, 10 minutes before the rice is finished cooking (they will cook in the rice). Alternatively, you can saute them with butter then add 10 minutes before rice is done.

***Optional Variation 3: Adding Parmesan Cheese- a great variation if you are not pairing it with seafood. About 10 minutes before the rice has finished cooking, add shredded, high quality parmesan to the rice.
Buon appetito!

Chicken Entrees

Chicken Parmigiana

Boneless chicken breast gets breaded, deep fried, and baked with marinara sauce and melted mozzarella. This chicken parm recipe was such a huge seller at the store and it s the dish people tell me they miss the most. The recipe came straight from my father's Villa Vespa kitchen. To this day, it's still the best chicken parm I've ever had.

Menu Planning

Serves: 4 people

Serves Well With:
- Spaghetti or Ziti
- Haricots Verts with Roasted Red Peppers and Garlic (page 56)
- Spinach Alla Villa Vespa (p.53)

TIMELINE

Prep Time		40 minutes (not including time to make Villa Vespa Marinara Sauce)
Cook Time	+	20 minutes
Total Time to Serving		**1 hour**

INGREDIENTS

Measurement	Ingredient	Special Instructions/Notes
4 6oz	Boneless chicken breasts (preferably small)	
1 C.	All-purpose flour or gluten-free flour	
4	Eggs	Lightly beaten
2 C.	Breadcrumbs (unseasoned)	
6 C.	Canola Oil	
	Salt	To taste
6 C.	Villa Vespa Marinara Sauce	Recipe on page 13; 1 C. to bake chicken plus additional sauce for serving
4 C.	Good quality mozzarella	Shredded
4 oz	Good quality parmesan or romano cheese	Grated
½ lb.	Pasta of Choice	I love to use Spaghetti or Ziti

EQUIPMENT

Name of Equipment	Special Instructions/Notes
Plastic wrap or one-gallon ziplock bag	
Meat pounder or mallet (in a pinch, you can also use the side of a hammer)	
Three separate shallow dishes or pie plates	
Large frying pan or wok	
13 x 9.5 inch Casserole Dish	
Large pot	For cooking pasta of choice

DIRECTIONS

Step 1

Preheat the oven to 350 degrees.

Step 2

Put a piece of plastic wrap on a cutting board. Place the pieces of chicken on top of the plastic wrap, smooth side up, and top with another layer of plastic wrap. This will make it easier to pound the chicken. You can place the chicken in a ziplock bag.

Step 3

Using a meat pounder, mallet, or side of a hammer if a mallet is not available, lightly pound the chicken to ¼ inch thick. You want to make sure the chicken is thin and even so they will fry quickly and cook evenly.

Step 4

Take three separate shallow dishes or pie plates, and place the flour, eggs, and breadcrumbs each into their own dish. Taking one chicken breast at a time, lightly dredge in the flour dish. Then dip the chicken in the egg wash, making sure to cover both sides. Next, place the chicken into breadcrumbs, again covering both sides, lightly pat chicken until breadcrumbs stick. Repeat with all the chicken.

Step 5

To prepare the oil for frying, first pour the oil in a large frying pan or wok over medium-high heat. Make sure you have enough oil in the pan so that the chicken will float. You don't want the chicken to touch the bottom of the pan. Before adding the chicken make sure the oil is hot enough. You can check the temperature by dipping a fork into the eggs and dropping a tiny bit into the oil. If it starts to cook, the oil is ready. Don't let the oil get too hot, or the chicken will cook too fast and may burn.

Step 6

Fry the chicken 2-3 pieces at a time, being sure not to crowd the pan. Cook the chicken about 5 minutes per side, or until golden brown, then place the chicken on a paper towel lined plate and sprinkle with salt.

Step 7

To assemble the chicken in the casserole dish, first lay a thin layer of marinara sauce on the bottom of the dish, about 1 C. This will keep the chicken from sticking to the pan. Next, lay the chicken on top of the marinara sauce. The chicken pieces may touch or overlap slightly.

Step 8

Atop each piece of chicken, sprinkle mozzarella and parmesan cheese. Place the dish into the oven and bake for 20 minutes. While the chicken is baking, cook the pasta following the cooking instructions on the package,making sure to add a generous amount of salt to the water while it is heating up. Heat additional marinara sauce to serve with dinner. Plate the chicken, pasta, and marinara sauce and enjoy!

Buon appetito!

Chicken Piccata or Veal Piccata

Thinly pounded meat in a rich, buttery lemon sauce. At the takeout store, I once had a customer order a family size of this dish for the first time. The next time she returned, she told me she loved it so much she could literally bathe in it. I love to serve this on a bed of spinach with a generous amount of sauce.

Before You Get Started

I prefer making this dish with white wine, but in a pinch you can completely substitute it with chicken broth.

Menu Planning

Serves: 4 people

Serves Well With:
- Cooked spinach (or lightly steamed vegetable such as asparagus or green beans)
- Pasta of choice
- Garlic bread (p.50)

TIMELINE

Prep Time	30 minutes
Cook Time	20 minutes
Total Time to Serving	**50 minutes**

INGREDIENTS

Measurement	Ingredient	Special Instructions/Notes
4 6oz	Chicken breasts	
¼ C.	Vegetable oil	For frying
1 C. + 2 Tbsp.	All-purpose flour or Gluten-free flour	1 C. for dredging raw chicken; 2 Tbsp. for making sauce
3 large	Eggs	Lightly beaten
16 ounces	Spinach	
½ lb	Butter	
2 tsp.	Salt	
1 tsp.	Pepper	
½ C.	White wine or chicken broth	
1 Tbsp	Capers	Rinsed
1	Large lemons	2 Tbsp freshly squeezed, 4 thin slices cut into rounds
2 Tbsp	Fresh parsley	Chopped

EQUIPMENT

Name of Equipment	Special Instructions/Notes
Plastic wrap or one-gallon ziplock bag	
Meat pounder or mallet (in a pinch, you can also use the side of a hammer)	
2 shallow dishes or pie plates	
2 medium saute pans	
12-inch saucepan	

DIRECTIONS

Step 1

First, prepare the chicken by putting a piece of plastic wrap on a cutting board. Place the pieces of chicken on top of the plastic wrap, smooth side up, and top with another layer of plastic wrap. This will make it easier to pound the chicken. You can place the chicken in a ziplock bag.

Step 2

Using a meat pounder, mallet, or side of a hammer if a mallet is not available, lightly pound the chicken to ¼ inch thick. You want to make sure the chicken is thin and even so they will fry quickly and cook evenly.

Step 3

Next, place a medium saute pan over medium heat and add the oil. Prepare 1 C. flour in one shallow dish or pie plate, and crack and lightly beat the eggs in a second shallow dish or pie plate.

Step 4

To cook the chicken, lightly flour the chicken then place in egg wash. Place the chicken in the pan one to two at a time, depending on the size of the skillet. Do not crowd the chicken. Cook for 5 minutes per side, or until golden brown. Turn down the heat if the chicken is cooking too fast. Once the chicken is cooked, place it on a plate off to the side and sprinkle lightly with salt. Discard the flour and egg mixtures.

Step 5

Next, cook the spinach. In a second saute pan, add 2 inches of water and a pinch of salt. Bring the water to a boil. Slowly add the spinach and cook until wilted, about 10 minutes. Drain the water and squeeze the remaining water out of the spinach. Place spinach on a cutting board and roughly chop so the pieces aren't too big.

Step 6

Return the dried pan to the stove and over low heat, add 1 Tbsp butter. After the butter melts, add the chopped spinach, 1 tsp salt, and 1 tsp pepper. Stir the spinach, and keep warm until serving.

Step 7

To make the sauce, melt the rest of the butter in a 12-inch saucepan over medium-low heat. Slowly sprinkle in 2 Tbsp flour, whisking as you add. Continue to whisk flour and butter together for 5 minutes. Do not let the butter get brown. Pour white wine or chicken broth into the cooked butter and flour mixture. Heat the mixture until it thickens- if you want the sauce thicker, add more butter, for a thinner sauce, add more liquid. Add the rinsed capers. Squeeze 2 Tbsp. lemon juice into the sauce. Remove from heat, add the parsley.

Step 8

To assemble your dish: Put the spinach on four separate plates or on a large platter. Lay the chicken on top of the spinach. Pour the sauce on top of the chicken. Finish with a slice of lemon atop each chicken breast. Enjoy!

Buon appetito!

Chicken Alla Villa Vespa

This was one of our signature dishes at the restaurant. I'm not sure who originally came up with the recipe, but I have yet to see it anywhere else. In the dish, thinly pounded chicken gets sauteed with white, button mushrooms and sweet, roasted red peppers. Served with a light white wine & butter sauce, it hits all the notes for creaminess and tanginess.

Menu Planning

Serves: 4 people

Prep Time		40 minutes
Cook Time	+	30 minutes
Total Time to Serving		**1 hour, 10 minutes**

Measurement	Ingredient	Special Instructions/Notes
4 6oz	Chicken breasts	
	Water	
4 C. / 16 ounce	Fresh Spinach	
	Salt	To taste
	Pepper	To taste
1 C. + 1 Tbsp.	All-purpose flour	You can substitute almond flour for a gluten-free alternative; 1 C. to dredge the chicken, 1 Tbsp. for the sauce
4	Eggs	Lightly beaten
¼ C.	Canola Oil	For frying
½ lb	Salted butter	
4 C.	White button mushrooms	Sliced
⅓ C.	Jarred roasted red peppers	Chopped
½ C.	White wine or chicken broth	
⅓ C.	Fresh parsley	Chopped

EQUIPMENT

Name of Equipment	Special Instructions/Notes
Plastic wrap or one-gallon ziplock bag	
Meat pounder or mallet (in a pinch, you can also use the side of a hammer)	
6-8 qt. stockpot or wok	
2 shallow dishes or pie plates	
12-inch saute pan	

DIRECTIONS

Step 1

First, pound the chicken- put a piece of plastic wrap on a cutting board. Place the pieces of chicken on top of the plastic wrap, smooth side up, and top with another layer of plastic wrap. This will make it easier to pound the chicken. Using a meat pounder, mallet or the side of a hammer, lightly pound the chicken to ¼ inch thick. You want to make sure the chicken is thin and even so it will fry quickly and cook evenly.

Step 2

To cook fresh spinach, place 4-inches of water in a stock pot or wok over high heat and add a pinch of salt. Bring to a boil then add the spinach, a little at a time, to let it cook down. Cook for 4 minutes, then remove from heat and drain the spinach. Squeeze out all the excess water from the spinach. Return it to the pan, with the burner off. Add salt and pepper, and put a lid on it to keep warm.

Step 3

In a shallow dish or pie plate, add 1 C. flour. In a second shallow dish or pie plate, add 4 eggs, lightly beaten. Heat the oil in a 12-inch saute pan over medium-high heat. Wait until the oil is hot before cooking the chicken. You can check the oil temperature by dipping a fork into the egg mixture and letting it fall into the oil. If it cooks, you are ready to start on the chicken. If not, be patient and let it heat further! To cook the chicken, first dredge one chicken breast in the flour, shaking off any excess. Next, dip the chicken into the egg mixture and carefully lay it into the pan of hot oil. Prepare a second chicken breast the same way, flouring and dipping into the egg mixture, before laying it in the pan beside the first piece. Only cook 2 pieces per batch, do not overcrowd the pan. Cook chicken for 5 minutes, then using a pair of tongs, turn it over in the pan and cook for another 5 minutes. Once the chicken is cooked, set it aside on a plate, and lightly sprinkle salt. Continue cooking all the chicken in batches using the same method.

Step 4

To make the sauce, first wipe all the oil out of the saute pan and place it back on the burner over medium heat. Add the butter and allow it to melt. Then add the mushrooms and roasted red peppers and cook for 3 minutes. Add 1 Tbsp. flour by sprinkling it around the pan and whisk to incorporate it, cooking for another 3 minutes. Add white wine or chicken broth and cook 5 minutes more. This sauce will thicken as it continues to cook. If it is too thick, add a touch more liquid. If it's too thin, add 2 tsp butter.

Step 5

When the sauce is ready, you can plate the dish. First, dish the cooked spinach, and top with the chicken. Pour the sauce over everything. You may either plate it on individual plates or on a large serving platter. Garnish with parsley, and extra salt and pepper to taste.

Buon appetito!

Spaghetti Caruso

A classic Italian dish- in our version, chicken livers are lightly dredged in flour and sauteed with onions, mushrooms, garlic, and cooking sherry, before stewing in the marinara sauce. Then everything is served over a bed of spaghetti. If you're a chicken liver lover, you are going to adore this. If you aren't an adventurous eater, I implore you to try this recipe. You won't regret it.

Before You Get Started

If your chicken livers are fresh and you have more than you need for the recipe, they can be frozen for later use.

Menu Planning

Serves: 2 people

TIMELINE

Prep Time		30 minutes (does not include time to make Villa Vespa Marinara Sauce)
Cook Time	+	30 minutes
Total Time to Serving		**1 hour**

INGREDIENTS

Measurement	Ingredient	Special Instructions/Notes
¼ lb.	Spaghetti or linguine	
3 Tbsp.	Olive Oil	
2 Tbsp.	Flour	
2 C.	Chicken Livers	Cleaned and halved
½	Medium yellow onion	
1 tsp.	Salt	
1 tsp.	Pepper	
1 Tbsp.	Fresh garlic	Chopped
6	White button mushrooms	
½ C.	Cooking sherry	
3 C.	Villa Vespa Marinara Sauce	Recipe on page 13
½ tsp	Italian seasoning	
¼ C.	Fresh parsley (optional)	Chopped

EQUIPMENT

Name of Equipment	Special Instructions/Notes
4-6 quart stockpot	For cooking the pasta
Strainer or colander	
Shallow dish or pie plate	
9-inch saute pan with lid	

DIRECTIONS

Step 1

Put a large stockpot on the stove and add enough water to cover your pasta. Add a generous amount of salt and bring the water to a boil. Cook the pasta according to the directions on the box or package. When it's done cooking, drain it into a strainer or colander. Add 1 Tbsp olive oil and toss to prevent it from sticking together.

Step 2

Measure the flour into a shallow dish or on a plate. Dredge the pieces of chicken liver in the flour on both sides, then set aside.

Step 3

Place 2 Tbsp olive oil in a 9-inch saute pan over medium-high. Add the onions and cook for 4 minutes while stirring. Add in the chicken livers, cooking for 4 minutes on each side. Season with a little salt and pepper. Stir in the garlic and mushrooms, cook for 5 minutes.

Step 4

Pour the cooking sherry into the pan and cook for 5 minutes. Add marinara sauce and Italian seasoning, top with a lid and simmer over low heat for 10 minutes. Taste and add extra salt and pepper as needed.

Step 5

To plate, serve pasta on a plate or in a nice pasta bowl. Top with sauce and chicken livers. Garnish with fresh parsley.

Buon appetito!

Chicken Marsala

Thinly pounded chicken, sauteed in a creamy mushroom white wine sauce. This dish is just so good. You can eat it with pasta, but I love it on top of steamed spinach, finished with salt and pepper. The creamy mushroom sauce covers everything and makes all of it delicious.

Prep Time	30 minutes
Cook Time	+ 20 minutes
Total Time to Serving	**50 minutes**

Before You Get Started

- The marsala wine is a very important ingredient in this recipe- it's not chicken marsala without it! If you want to remove the alcohol, just take a match and light the wine on fire to burn off the liquor. Just be careful as it will flame up. Use a lid to put out the fire after cooking.

- This is a pretty fast recipe once the chicken starts cooking. Make your pasta or vegetable prior to chicken, so it's hot and ready to be plated as soon as the chicken is done.

INGREDIENTS

Measurement	Ingredient	Special Instructions/Notes
4 6-oz	Chicken breasts	
½ lb.	Fresh spinach, asparagus, or green beans	(pasta may also be used as a side, tagliatelle is good here)
1 C. + 1 tsp.	Flour	
3	Eggs	Lightly beaten
1 C.	Canola Oil	For frying
¼ lb.	Butter	
1 C.	Small white mushrooms	Sliced
1 C.	Sweet marsala wine	Purchase at the liquor store
1 pint	Heavy Cream	
2 Tbsp.	Parsley (fresh)	Chopped

EQUIPMENT

Name of Equipment	Special Instructions/Notes
One-gallon ziplock bag or plasic wrap	
Meat pounder/mallet or the side of a hammer	
2 shallow dishes or pie plates	
12-inch Saute pan	

Menu Planning

Serves: 4 people

Serves Well With:
- Pasta of choice
- Spinach
- Asparagus
- Green Beans

DIRECTIONS

Step 1

Put a piece of plastic wrap on a cutting board. Place the pieces of chicken on top of the plastic wrap, smooth side up, and top with another layer of plastic wrap. This will make it easier to pound the chicken. You can place the chicken in a ziplock bag.

Step 2

Using a meat pounder, mallet, or side of a hammer if a mallet is not available, lightly pound the chicken to ¼ inch thick. You want to make sure the chicken is thin and even so they will fry quickly and cook evenly.

Step 3

Cook your pasta or vegetable of choice. If you're making pasta, cook according to the directions on the box or package. After draining it, while keeping it warm, add 1 Tbsp. olive oil to keep it from sticking together. If you're making vegetables such as spinach, asparagus, or green beans, lightly steam them in a small saute pan with simmering water and a pinch of salt. Cook for 5 minutes then drain and keep warm while cooking chicken.

Step 4

Place the flour in a shallow dish or pie plate. Place the lightly beaten eggs into another shallow dish or pie plate.

Step 5

To cook the chicken: Heat the oil in a saute pan over medium heat. Dredge each chicken piece into the flour, then dip into the egg mixture and place in the hot skillet. Only place one or two chicken pieces in the skillet at a time so you don't crowd the chicken. Proceed to cook the chicken on both sides, about 3-5 minutes per side, until golden brown in color. Once cooked, place the chicken aside on the plate or platter. Finish cooking the remaining chicken pieces. Once all the chicken is cooked, begin to make the sauce.

Step 6

To make the sauce: Discard the oil from the saute pan that you cooked the chicken in. Wipe the pan clean of any remaining oil. Place the pan back on the stove over low heat and add the butter. Once the butter is melted, add the mushrooms and sprinkle in 1 tsp flour. Whisk to incorporate the flour, cooking for 5 minutes.

Step 7

Once the mushrooms are soft, add the marsala wine. Cook for 2 minutes. Add the heavy cream and cook for 5 minutes more. The sauce should be thick and very fragrant.

Step 8

Assemble your platter or individual plates- dish the pasta or vegetable first, then lay the chicken over it. Then pour the sauce and garnish with parsley.

Buon appetito!

Chicken Cacciatore

A baked chicken dish wherein onion, mushroom, and garlic reduce into a gravy-like sauce. The addition of cooking sherry adds sweetness and depth. This dish is easy and was a big seller at both the restaurant and the store.

Before You Get Started

The sherry is a very important ingredient in this recipe. If you want to remove all the alcohol, place the sherry in the saute pan with the chicken, then take a match and light it on fire. This will burn off the liquor, but be careful as it will briefly flame.

Menu Planning

Serves: 4 people

Serves Well With:
- Pasta
- Vegetables

TIMELINE

Prep Time		30 minutes
Cook Time	+	45 minutes
Total Time to Serving		1 hour, 15 minutes

INGREDIENTS

Measurement	Ingredient	Special Instructions/Notes
¼ C.	Vegetable Oil	
1 C.	Flour	Regular or gluten-free
4 6-8oz	Chicken breasts	Or, you may use 8-12 chicken tenders
1	Medium yellow onion	Diced
6	Medium white mushrooms	Sliced
1 Tbsp	Fresh garlic	Chopped
¼ C.	Cooking Sherry or sweet sherry	
3 C.	Marinara Sauce	See recipe on page 13

EQUIPMENT

Name of Equipment	Special Instructions/Notes
4-inch deep saute pan with oven proof handle or 11-qt. dutch oven	
Shallow dish or pie plate	

DIRECTIONS

Step 1

Preheat the oven to 350 degrees. In a large saute pan or dutch oven, heat the oil over medium heat. Measure the flour into a shallow dish or pie plate.

Step 2

Rinse and dry the chicken breast. Dredge into the flour then shake off any excess flour.

Step 3

Taking care not to crowd the pan, carefully lay the chicken into the hot oil and cook until brown on both sides, about 3 minutes per side. Dredge and cook in two batches if necessary.

Step 4

Remove chicken from the pan and set aside. Once all the chicken has been cooked, pour half of the oil out of the pan, leaving just enough to fry the vegetables.

Step 5

Set the pan over medium heat. Add the onions to the oil and saute for 4-5 minutes, until golden brown, stirring occasionally.

Step 6

Next add the mushrooms and garlic, cook 4-5 minutes, until the garlic is golden and mushrooms have softened. Add cooking sherry and let it simmer and reduce for 3 minutes.

Step 7

Add the marinara sauce to the pan and add the chicken breasts back in, stirring to mix. Place the pan or dutch oven in the oven and bake for 25 minutes.

Buon appetito!

Chicken Pot Pie

started selling this dish at the takeout store and it became extremely popular- we literally couldn't keep it on our shelves. One important lesson I learned from my dad was to always add a soup base to the broth for flavor. Although not traditional to the dish, I decided to add potatoes to give it an extra heartiness during the cold winters in Lake Placid.

Before You Get Started

This recipe can easily be doubled- one to eat and the other to freeze.

Menu Planning

Serves: 4 people

Serves Well With:
- Puff Pastry or Biscuits
- Wide egg noodles
- A nice side salad made with Balsamic Vinaigrette (p.72) or Caesar Dressing (p.74)

TIMELINE

Prep Time		45 minutes
Cook Time	+	55 minutes
Total Time to Serving		**1 hour, 40 minutes**

INGREDIENTS

Measurement	Ingredient	Special Instructions/Notes
1 Small box	Puff pastry	
¼ C.	Olive oil	
1	Small yellow onion	Diced
2 Tbsp.	Fresh garlic	Chopped
3	Carrots	Peeled and sliced into thin circles
3	Celery Stalks	Diced
1 Tbsp.	Salt	
1 Tbsp.	Pepper	
6 6-oz	Chicken breasts	Cut into bite-size pieces
2	Large russet potatoes	Peeled and diced
1 tsp.	Dried basil	
1 ½ lb.	Butter	
2 Tbsp.	Flour	
2	Bay leaves	
32 oz	Good quality chicken broth	
1 tsp.	Good quality chicken base/ bouillon	
8 oz	Frozen peas	
½ C.	Heavy Cream	

EQUIPMENT

Name of Equipment	Special Instructions/Notes
Dutch oven or saucepan	

DIRECTIONS

Step 1

Cook the puff pastry according to directions on the box.

Step 2

Coat the bottom of a dutch oven or saucepan with the olive oil. Heat oil over medium heat, and add the chopped onion. Saute until golden brown, 5 minutes.

Step 3

Add the garlic and cook until golden brown, about 3 minutes. Then add the carrots and celery. Stir and let sweat for 5 minutes.

Step 4

Add the chicken, salt, and pepper to the pot. Stir and cook thoroughly, about 5-10 minutes

Step 5

Add dried basil, butter, and flour. Stir and let cook for 5 minutes more, then add the bay leaves. Cover the mixture with the chicken broth, add the chicken base, and simmer for 15-20 minutes, stirring occasionally.

Step 6

Slowly add in the heavy cream. Continue to cook and stir until it is thick and creamy, about 20 minutes.

Step 7

To serve, place the cooked puff pastry on your plate. Top with the chicken pot pie and enjoy!

Buon appetito!

Children's Chicken Fingers with French Fries

This was a hit at the restaurant for both kids and adults! This boneless chicken recipe is super easy with lots of flavor.

Serves: 2 kids

TIMELINE

Prep Time	15 minutes
Cook Time	+ 25 minutes
Total Time to Serving	40 minutes

INGREDIENTS

Measurement	Ingredient	Special Instructions/Notes
1	Small bag of your favorite frozen french fries	
1 C.	All-purpose flour	You can substitute Almond flour for a gluten-free alternative
3	Eggs	Lightly beaten
¼ C.	Sesame seeds	
1 Tbsp.	Salt	
1 Tbsp.	Pepper (optional)	
3 C.	Vegetable or Canola Oil	For frying
6-8	Chicken tenders or 2 6-ounce chicken breasts	If using chicken breasts, slice each breast lengthwise into 3 pieces
	Honey	For dipping or drizzling
	Ketchup	For dipping

EQUIPMENT

Name of Equipment	Special Instructions/Notes
2 baking sheets	
2 shallow dishes or pie plates	
8-quart wok or 8-quart saute pan with 2-inch deep sides	

DIRECTIONS

Step 1

Preheat the oven according to the directions on the french fry package and spread the fries out onto a baking sheet. While the oven is preheating, prepare the eggs by cracking them into a shallow dish or pie plate, then lightly beat them, and add salt, pepper (if desired), and sesame seeds. In a second shallow dish or pie plate, add the flour. Bake the french fries according to the directions on the package.

Step 2

When the french fries are 15 minutes from being done, heat the oil in a wok or saute pan over medium-high heat. Before adding the chicken to the oil, make sure it is hot enough. You can check the oil temperature by dipping a fork into the egg mixture and letting it drip in the oil. If it starts to immediately cook, the oil is ready.

Step 3

Dredge three pieces of chicken in the flour, shaking off any excess flour, then dip them into the egg mixture. Carefully place the dredged chicken into the hot oil. You don't want the chicken to cook too fast, so If you think it's too hot, you can turn the heat down slightly.

Step 4

Fry the chicken in the oil for 10 minutes, turning over halfway. When the first 3 pieces are done, lay them on the second baking sheet and proceed to dredge and fry the remainder of the chicken, no more than 3 pieces at a time so as to not crowd the pan.

Step 5

Once all the chicken has been placed on the baking sheet, place it in the oven to cook for an additional 5 minutes to ensure they are thoroughly cooked.

Step 6

Remove the chicken and french fries from the oven and sprinkle with salt to taste. Serve the chicken with a side of honey and the fries with a side of ketchup.

Buon appetito!

Grilled Balsamic Chicken

This was one of my dad's favorites, although he would make it using cornish game hen. Personally, I prefer the ease of chicken as there are far fewer tiny bones. The beauty of this dish is that most of the ingredients are probably already in your pantry. Marinating the chicken in a high quality balsamic glaze or aged balsamic vinegar takes it to another level.

Before You Get Started

- Balsamic glaze is a reduced balsamic vinegar you can find at certain grocery stores. It's thick and syrupy. If you can't find it, you can use aged balsamic vinegar.

- On different cuts of chicken- I prefer to make this with skin-on chicken breasts because the skin fries up nicely in the grill pan, but if boneless and skinless is your preference, go for it! For that matter, you can use any cut of chicken- breast, leg, or thigh, even a half chicken would work!

- I love to serve this with roasted brussels sprouts that have been sauteed with the same marinade. See the note at the bottom for how to cook brussels sprouts in this way.

Menu Planning

Serves: 4 people

Serves Well With:
- Brussels Sprouts (see note at the bottom for how to cook)
- Haricots Verts with Roasted Peppers & Garlic (p.56)
- Spinach Alla Villa Vespa (p.53)

TIMELINE

Prep Time		1 hour, 20 minutes
Cook Time	+	20 minutes
Total Time to Serving		**1 hour, 40 minutes**

INGREDIENTS

Measurement	Ingredient	Special Instructions/Notes
4 6-8oz	Chicken breasts (either with ribs, skin-on and boneless, or skinless and boneless)	
1 C.	Olive oil	
1 C.	Balsamic Vinegar	
1 Tbsp.	Balsamic glaze or aged balsamic vinegar	
1	Large lemon	Halved, one half sliced into rounds, the other half juiced
1 C.	Dry tarragon	
1 Tbsp	Salt	
1 Tbsp.	Pepper	
1 tsp.	Vegetable or Canola oil	

EQUIPMENT

Name of Equipment	Special Instructions/Notes
Baking sheet	
Parchment paper	
Medium baking dish	
Small bowl	
9-inch ridged cast-iron grill pan or cast-iron pan	

DIRECTIONS

Step 1

Preheat the oven to 300 degrees. Line a baking sheet with parchment paper. Lay the chicken breasts in a medium baking dish for marinating. In a small bowl, combine the olive oil, balsamic vinegar, balsamic glaze or aged balsamic vinegar, juice of half a lemon, tarragon, salt, and pepper. Pour the marinade over the chicken, making sure to coat all of it. Place plastic wrap on top of the pan and let the chicken rest for at least 1 hour. You can also put it in the refrigerator and let it rest overnight.

Step 2

Using a paper towel, wipe a cast-iron pan or grill pan with 1 tsp vegetable or canola oil to prevent sticking, and place it on a burner over medium-high heat. When the skillet is hot, remove two of the chicken breasts from the marinade and place them in the pan. Let them cook for 4 minutes on the first side then flip the pieces over. Pour ½ C. of the marinade from the dish into the pan. Cook the chicken and marinade for 4 minutes. When done, place the chicken on the lined baking sheet, and proceed to cook the remaining chicken.

Step 3

Once you've cooked all the chicken, put it in the oven to bake for 10 minutes, making sure it is cooked thoroughly. If you're using 6-ounce chicken breasts, they may not need the full 10 minutes. Use a meat thermometer to ensure it reaches an internal temperature of at least 165 degrees. Take the chicken out of the oven and serve with a slice of lemon on top. If you'd like, you can drizzle aged Balsamic or balsamic glaze over the top just before serving.

Buon appetito!

***Note:**To add a side of brussels sprouts, cook them in a saute pan with a bit of the marinade, then roast for 10 minutes. Serve alongside the chicken.

Meat Entrees

"The Godfather"- Spaghetti with Sausage, Peppers, and Onions

Another example of how the Villa Vespa marinara sauce really transforms, based on the ingredients you add to it. This dish strikes a nice balance between the sweet peppers and the hot Italian sausage. If you like it extra spicy, you can add a touch of crushed red pepper. This sauce in this dish becomes almost gravy-like as the peppers simmer and cook down.

Menu Planning

Serves: 4 people

Serves Well With:
- Risotto Milanese (p.98)
- Pasta of Choice (any pasta would be delicious)
- In a toasted sub roll, topped with cheese such as provolone

TIMELINE

Prep Time		40 minutes
Cook Time	+	35 minutes
Total Time to Serving		**1 hour, 15 minutes**

INGREDIENTS

Measurement	Ingredient	Special Instructions/Notes
4	Italian hot sausage links	
¼ C.	Olive oil	
1	Medium yellow onion	Cut into strips
1	Red bell pepper	Cut into strips lengthwise
1	Yellow bell pepper	Cut into strips lengthwise
1 Tbsp	Fresh garlic	Chopped
4 C.	Villa Vespa Marinara Sauce	Recipe on page 13
1 tsp.	Italian seasoning	
	Salt & Pepper	
1 splash	Red or white wine (if you have it handy)	
¼ C.	Fresh basil	Chopped

EQUIPMENT

Name of Equipment	Special Instructions/Notes
12-inch saute pan	

DIRECTIONS

Step 1

Preheat the oven to 350 degrees. Cook the sausage links for 20 minutes, then let cool. Once cooled, slice them in half, lengthwise.

Step 2

In a 12-inch saute pan over medium heat, add the olive oil. Add onions and peppers to the oil and saute for 10 minutes, stirring occasionally, until the vegetables have softened. Stir in the garlic, and cook for 3 minutes. Push the vegetables to the side and add the halved sausages, laying them open side down in the pan, cook for 5 minutes.

Step 3

Next add the marinara sauce, Italian seasoning, salt, and pepper, and wine. Stir everything together and cook over medium-low heat for 15 minutes. Add the fresh basil just before serving. Taste and add more salt and pepper as needed.

Buon appetito!

Veal Ragout

Tender veal diced and sauteed in oil and baked with marinara sauce, mushrooms, and onions. If you cannot find veal stew meat at the store, you can substitute beef stew meat.

Menu Planning

Serves: 6-8 people

Serves Well With:

- Pasta of Choice- preferably a thick noodle such as tagliatelle or fettuccine
- Rice
- Garlic Bread (p.50)

Garlic Bread (p.50)

TIMELINE

Prep Time	30 minutes
Cook Time	+ 2 hours, 30 minutes
Total Time to Serving	**3 hours**

INGREDIENTS

Measurement	Ingredient	Special Instructions/Notes
1 C.	All purpose flour	
3 lbs	Veal stew meat	
1 C.	Canola Oil	
1	Medium Yellow Onion	Diced
3 Tbsp.	Fresh garlic	Finely chopped
1 Tbsp.	Salt	
1 Tbsp.	Pepper	
1 tsp.	Italian Seasoning	
1 C.	Red Wine	
2 C.	Marinara Sauce	Recipe on page 13
16 ounces/ 2 C.	Beef Stock	
2 C.	White Mushrooms	Sliced
8 ounces	Frozen Peas	
½ C.	Fresh basil	Chopped

EQUIPMENT

Name of Equipment	Special Instructions/Notes
6-8 quart Dutch oven or oven-proof stock pot	

DIRECTIONS

Step 1

Lightly flour the veal stew pieces. Place a large dutch oven or oven-proof stock pot on the stove over medium-high heat. Add the canola oil to the pot, and let it heat. Once the oil is hot enough, fry the veal pieces, 4-5 minutes on each side. Take the meat out of the pan and set aside.

Step 2

Pour half the oil out of the pan, leaving about ½ cup. Add the diced onions to the oil and cook until golden brown, 5 minutes. Add the garlic and cook for 3 minutes more. When everything is golden brown, add the stew meat back in. Sprinkle in salt, pepper, and Italian seasoning.

Step 3

Stir in the red wine, and cook for 5 minutes. Then add the marinara sauce and beef stock. Cover the pan and put it in the oven for 2 hours, stirring occasionally. After one hour, add the mushrooms, peas, and fresh basil.

Buon appetito!

Spaghetti Carbonara

This is my daughter Emma's favorite pasta- while she was growing up we used to call it spaghetti, bacon, and eggs. It is fun and simple, and the best part is that most people already have all the ingredients in their refrigerator.

Menu Planning

Serves: 2 people

TIMELINE

Prep Time	30 minutes
Cook Time	+ 15 minutes
Total Time to Serving	**45 minutes**

INGREDIENTS

Measurement	Ingredient	Special Instructions/Notes
3	Eggs	Lightly beaten
¼ C.	Half and half	
3 Tbsp + 1 tsp.	Olive oil	
1 C.	Good quality bacon	Diced, uncooked
⅓ lb.	Dried pasta, such as linguine or spaghetti	
1 C.	Onion	Diced
3 Tbsp	Fresh Garlic	Diced
½ C.	Parmesan cheese, Romano cheese, or a blend	Grated
¼ C.	Parsley	Chopped
	Salt & pepper	To taste

EQUIPMENT

Name of Equipment	Special Instructions/Notes
Large saute pan	Big enough to hold the pasta

DIRECTIONS

Step 1

Combine the eggs and half and half in a small bowl and set aside. In a large saute pan over medium heat, add the olive oil and bacon. Cook for 10 minutes, stirring occasionally. While the bacon is cooking, bring a large pot of salted water to a boil to cook the pasta. Cook the pasta as directed on the box then drain and toss with 1 tsp olive oil so it doesn't stick together.

Step 2

Add onions to the bacon and saute for 5 minutes. Then stir in the garlic, cook 3 minutes more. If the garlic is starting to burn, you may add a splash of half and half to the pan.

Step 3

Add the pasta to the bacon mixture. Add the egg mixture to the pan and toss to coat the pasta and gently heat. Do not let the mixture get too hot, or the eggs will scramble.

Step 4

Stir continuously until it warms, it should reach 180 degrees, you may check with a thermometer. Add cheese, fresh parsley, and finish with salt and pepper. Toss once more then serve!

Buon appetito!

A Little Spicy Italian Meatball

Beef, hot sausage, and eggs render these meatballs juicy, spicy, and tender. Since they are pretty labor intensive, I've scaled the recipe so it makes a large batch. This way, you can easily freeze them for later enjoyment. I love meatballs for their versatility- you can eat them in a sub for lunch, with pasta for dinner, or they are delicious on their own if you need a little snack.

Before You Get Started

This is one of the more time-intensive recipes, so make sure you plan accordingly. A 3oz ice cream scoop with a release makes the process faster and easier.

Menu Planning

Makes: 33 meatballs

Serves Well With:
- Villa Vespa Marinara Sauce (p.13)
- Your pasta of choice
- Sub roll, marinara, and cheese

Villa Vespa Marinara Sauce (p.13)

TIMELINE

Prep Time	40 minutes
Cook Time	30 minutes
Rest Time +	10 minutes
Total Time to Serving	**1 hour, 20 minutes**

INGREDIENTS

Measurement	Ingredient	Special Instructions/Notes
2 C.	French Bread	Stale or dry, Cut into small pieces
3	Eggs	
2 Tbsp.	Italian seasoning	
2 Tbsp.	Dried basil	
2 Tbsp.	Salt	
2 Tbsp.	Pepper	
¼ C.	Olive oil	
1	Medium Yellow Onion	Finely chopped
2	Stalks of Celery	Finely chopped
¼ C.	Fresh Garlic	Finely chopped
5 lb.	Ground beef	
1 lb.	Hot Italian Sausage	
½ C.	Breadcrumbs	
½ C.	Water	

EQUIPMENT

Name of Equipment	Special Instructions/Notes
6-8 inch saute pan	
2 deep baking sheets	Sides should be at least 2 inches deep
Parchment paper	
Food processor or blender	
3-oz ice cream scoop (or ⅓ measuring cup)	

DIRECTIONS

Step 1

Preheat the oven to 325 degrees. Line 2 baking sheets with parchment paper.

Step 2

Cut french bread into small pieces and place into a bowl. Add eggs, the Italian seasoning basil, 1 Tbsp. salt, and 1 Tbsp. pepper. Stir together and let soak.

Step 3

Place a 6-8 inch saute over medium-high heat and add the olive oil. Add the onion and celery To the pan and saute for 15 minutes, stirring occasionally. Add the garlic and stir cooking for 5 minutes more. Take the pan off the heat and allow it to cool.

Step 4

Combine warm vegetable mixture and soaked bread mixture in a food processor. Pulse 10 times- you may also use a blender or simply crush with your hands.

Step 5

In a large bowl, combine the ground beef and sausage, mixing well with your hands to combine. Add 1 Tbsp salt, 1 Tbsp. pepper, and the mixture from the food processor. Using your hands, mix well again. Sprinkle in breadcrumbs and mix again. Set the mixture aside for 10 minutes to rest. If after 10 minutes you notice that the meatballs are too moist for rolling, you can add a little more breadcrumbs.

Step 6

Using the ice cream scoop or ⅓ measuring cup, scoop the meat mixture onto the baking sheets. After all the mixture has been measured out, roll the individual meatballs by hand to compress the meat and make them round.

Step 7

Add ½ C. water to the bottom of the baking sheet before cooking to retain moisture while cooking. Cook meatballs until they are solid to the touch, about 20-30 minutes. Either serve immediately, or if freezing, first pour out excess water and oil from the tray into a metal can (I usually pour it into the empty tomato can). Allow meatballs to sit and cool. After they cool, leave them in the refrigerator overnight, covered. Freeze the next day.

Buon appetito!

Old World Lasagne with a Hearty Bolognese

This is our 40-year-old lasagne recipe. Nothing has changed since my dad first started serving it as a special back at the restaurant, and for good reason. I think this lasagna really stands out because of all the layers. You have the creaminess from the Bechamel, the saltiness from the ricotta and parmesan, the mild spice from the Bolognese, and the gooey cheesiness from the mozzarella. It takes a little time and effort to make, but it does serve a large crowd and makes really great leftovers.

Before You Get Started

This is an advanced recipe with a lot of preparation and several steps-have the Bechamel Sauce (p.20), Ricotta Cheese Mixture (p.25), Villa Vespa Marinara Sauce (p.13), and the Bolognese (p.16) prepared in advance to speed up the process.

Menu Planning

Serves: 6-8 people

Serves Well With:
- Side Salad
- Garlic Bread (p.50)
- Your favorite bottle of red wine

TIMELINE

Prep Time	30 minutes (not including the time to make the sauces)
Cook Time	+ 45 minutes
Total Time to Serving	1 hours, 15 minutes

INGREDIENTS

Measurement	Ingredient	Special Instructions/Notes
3 C.	Bechamel Sauce	Recipe on page 20
32 ounces	Ricotta Cheese Mixture	Recipe on page 25, double the recipe for the right quantity
4 C.	Villa Vespa Marinara Sauce	Recipe on page 13
4 C.	Bolognese Sauce	Recipe on page 16
	Olive oil spray or butter	(such as Pam™)
18 oz	Oven ready lasagna noodles	I purchase 2 9-ounce boxes
16 oz	Shredded Mozzarella	Use good, high quality cheese
1 C.	Pecorino Romano Cheese	Grated

EQUIPMENT

Name of Equipment	Special Instructions/Notes
8 x 10 x 2 inch oven/casserole pan	

DIRECTIONS

Step 1

Make the Bechamel Sauce (p.20), Ricotta Cheese Mixture (p.25), Villa Vespa Marinara Sauce (p.13), and the Bolognese (p.16) according to their individual recipes. Set each aside until ready to assemble the lasagna.

Step 2

Preheat the oven to 350 degrees. When you're ready to assemble the lasagna, first grease the bottom of a casserole pan with oil spray or butter. Then, add a thin layer of Villa Vespa Marinara Sauce. Add 2 C. shredded mozzarella and spread evenly. Next, add 2 layers of pasta- I like an extra layer here to create more structure. Add all of the ricotta mixture and spread over the top. Add a layer of lasagna noodles. Then pour in all of the bolognese sauce. Add another pasta layer, then pour on the bechamel sauce, spread evenly. Add another layer of pasta.

Step 3

Finally, add one more layer of marinara sauce, and top with salt, pepper, romano cheese, and mozzarella cheese. Spread evenly. Wipe the edges clean, and bake in the oven for 40 minutes, until it is hot and bubbling. The cheese should be melted but not brown.

Buon appetito!

Baked Ziti

This is by far one of my favorite dishes to make on a cold winter's day (and we have a lot of those in upstate NY!). Although it utilizes a different pasta, all the filling ingredients are the same as the Old World Lasagne recipe. If you make the Bechamel (p.20), Marinara (p.13), Bolognese (p.16), and Ricotta mixture (p.25) ahead of time, this casserole will be a breeze.

Before you get started

I repeat, I highly recommend you make the Bechamel (p.20), Ricotta Cheese Mixture (p.25), Villa Vespa Marinara sauce (p.13), and Bolognese (p.16) ahead of time. It will speed up the process significantly.

Menu Planning

Serves: 4-6 people

Serves Well With:
- Garlic Bread (p.50)
- A nice salad with Balsamic Dressing (p.72) or Caesar Dressing (p.74)
- A side of Haricots Verts with Roasted Peppers and Garlic (p.56)

TIMELINE

Prep Time		40 minutes (Not including the time to prepare Marinara Sauce or Bolognese)
Cook Time		45 minutes
Rest Time	+	30 minutes
Total Time to Serving		**2 hours, 15 minutes**

INGREDIENTS

Measurement	Ingredient	Special Instructions/Notes
4 C.	Villa Vespa Marinara Sauce	Recipe on page 13
½ lb	Penne Rigate	I prefer De Cecco brand, cooked according to directions on the box
2 C.	Ricotta Cheese Mixture	Recipe on page 25
2 C.	Bechamel Sauce	Recipe on page 20
2 C.	Bolognese	You may substitute with marinara sauce if you prefer a vegetarian dish
1 Tbsp.	Italian seasoning	
1 C.	Shredded mozzarella	Use a high-quality name brand
1 C.	Good quality Parmesan or Romano Cheese	Grated
1 tsp.	Salt	
1 tsp.	Pepper	

EQUIPMENT

Name of Equipment	Special Instructions/Notes
9.5 x 9.5 x 2.5 casserole pan	

DIRECTIONS

Step 1

Preheat the oven to 350 degrees. In a casserole pan, spread a layer of marinara sauce on the bottom, about 2 cups.

Step 2

To assemble the casserole, on top of the marinara base, add a layer of penne noodles to cover the bottom. Then add all the Ricotta Cheese Mixture and smooth it out. Pour all the bechamel sauce on top of the ricotta mixture. Next, add another layer of penne pasta to cover. Then, pour all the bolognese on top of the pasta. Add another layer of the ziti and sprinkle Italian seasoning. Finally, pour the remaining marinara sauce. Top it off with the shredded mozzarella and grated parmesan or romano. If any ziti noodles are poking out of the sides, simply tuck them in and cover them with marinara.

Step 3

Place the ziti in the oven and bake for 40 minutes. The cheese on top should be golden and bubbly.

Buon appetito!

Seafood Entrees

Fresh Fillet of Sole

Tender white fish gets lightly sauteed and served with a lemony butter sauce, alongside asparagus or spinach. Sole is a light and delicate fish with a texture firmer than tilapia or cod. It has a very mild flavor, making this a great seafood dish for those that don't typically love seafood.

Menu Planning

Serves: 2 people

Prep Time	20 minutes
Cook Time	+ 30 minutes
Total Time to Serving	**50 minutes**

INGREDIENTS

Measurement	Ingredient	Special Instructions/Notes
12	Asparagus	Cut off 1-inch from bottoms and skin peeled with a vegetable peeler; You may substitute asparagus with 4 C. fresh spinach)
2 6oz or 4 4oz	Fillets of Sole	Serve each person either one 6oz fillet or two 4oz fillets
¼ C. + 1 tsp.	All-purpose flour	You can substitute Almond flour for a gluten-free alternative
2	Eggs	Lightly beaten
3 Tbsp.	Canola Oil	For frying
1	Lemon	
¼ lb.	Butter	
½ C.	White wine or vegetable broth	
2 Tbsp.	Fresh Parsley	Chopped
	Salt & Pepper	

EQUIPMENT

Name of Equipment	Special Instructions/Notes
6-8-inch saute pan	
2 shallow dishes or pie plates	
12-inch saute pan	
Metal spatula	
Metal tongs	

DIRECTIONS

Step 1

In a 6-8 inch saute pan, bring 1 C. water to a boil. Steam the asparagus or spinach, cooking for 5 minutes. Drain from the pan and either transfer back to the pan or to a bowl. Add 2 Tbsp. butter, salt, and pepper. Cover to keep warm and set aside.

Step 2

Pat the sole fillets dry with paper towels. In a shallow dish or pie plate, add ¼ C. flour. In a second shallow dish or pie plate, add the eggs. In a 12-inch saute pan, heat the oil over medium-high heat. Wait until the oil is hot before cooking the fish. You can check the oil temperature by dipping a fork into the egg mixture and letting it fall into the oil. If it cooks, the oil is ready. Be sure the oil does not get too hot, or the fish will burn.

Step 3

To cook the fish, first dredge one fillet in the flour, shaking off any excess flour. Then dip it in the egg mixture and carefully lay it into the pan of hot oil. Repeat with the second fillet.

Step 4

Have a good spatula and tongs ready to flip the fish. Cook the fish for 5 minutes on each side. After it's done cooking, transfer it to a plate and cover to keep warm while you make the sauce.

Step 5

To make the sauce, first cut the lemon in half. Slice one of the halves into rounds to use for garnish. Juice the other lemon half for the sauce.

Step 6

Drain all the oil from the saute pan and wipe clean with a paper towel. Allow the pan to cool slightly, as to not burn the butter when making the sauce. Return the pan to the stove over medium heat and add the butter. After the butter has melted, slowly sprinkle in 1 tsp flour, whisking as you add. Continue to whisk for 4 minutes.

Step 7

Slowly, begin to add the wine or broth to the pan. Add enough liquid to get the consistency you would like, the more wine/broth you add, the thinner the sauce will be. Add 1 Tbsp lemon juice and freshly chopped parsley, and stir to combine. Taste and add additional wine, broth, lemon juice, salt, and pepper if needed.

Step 8

To assemble the plates, arrange the asparagus/spinach on the plate next to the fillet of sole. Pour the sauce over everything and garnish with more parsley if desired.

Buon appetito!

Cod Livornese

This elegant dinner is really simple when you have your Villa Vespa Marinara Sauce already made. Fresh cod gets poached in a flavorful sauce made up of fresh garlic, sweet bell peppers, and marinara. I prefer to make it with cod and serve it with linguine, but you can use any meaty white fish and pasta of your choosing.

Menu Planning

Serves: 2 people

Serves Well With:
- Spinach Alla Villa Vespa (p.53)
- Garlic Bread (p.50)

TIMELINE

Prep Time		20 minutes (Not including time to make the Villa Vespa Marinara Sauce)
Cook Time	+	30 minutes
Total Time to Serving		50 minutes

INGREDIENTS

Measurement	Ingredient	Special Instructions/Notes
¼ C. + 1 tsp.	Olive oil	
½	Medium yellow onion	Sliced
½	Yellow or red bell pepper	Sliced lengthwise into strips
1 Tbsp	Fresh garlic	Chopped
3 C.	Villa Vespa Marinara Sauce	Recipe on page 13
½ C.	White wine, chicken broth, or vegetable broth	
2 8oz	Cod fillets (or any meaty, white fish)	
4 oz (¼ box)	Linguine (or other pasta of choice)	
¼ C.	Parsley	Freshly chopped

EQUIPMENT

Name of Equipment	Special Instructions/Notes
8-quart stock pot	
9-inch saute pan or saucepan with a lid	

DIRECTIONS

Step 1

Begin by bringing an 8-quart stockpot of salted water to a boil. This will be used to cook the pasta.

Step 2

While the water is heating, place a 9-inch saute pan or saucepan on the stove over medium heat and add ¼ C. olive oil. Then add the onions and peppers to the pan and cook for 5 minutes. Add the garlic and cook for another 5 minutes. Next add the marinara sauce and wine or broth, stir, and cook for 5 minutes more.

Step 3

Add the cod fillets on top of the sauce and cover with a lid. Bring the heat down to low and simmer for 10 minutes.

Step 4

While the cod is poaching, put the pasta in the boiling water and cook it according to the directions on the box or package. Once the pasta has cooked, drain it and add 1 tsp olive oil to prevent it from sticking. Don't let the pasta cool- the pasta and cod should be done around the same time.

Step 5

To assemble and serve, first take a plate and add the cooked pasta on one side. Place a cod fillet next to the pasta. Stir the sauce and ladle it over the pasta. Garnish with fresh parsley and serve!

Buon appetito!

Linguine with White Clam Sauce

A creamy, garlicky sauce for any seafood lover. For this recipe, feel free to add in any seafood you'd like. It's so simple that at the restaurant we made it to order.

Before You Get Started

- A few notes on clams- When you're dealing with canned clams, make sure to open the can and smell it before using. It should not smell like anything.

- To clean the fresh clams before using, make sure to submerge them in a big bowl of cold salted water and let them soak for at least 5 minutes, so they will expel any remaining sand. Scoop them out with a slotted spoon or fine mesh sieve, so you do not pour the sand back on top of them.

- Lastly, if any are open when you purchase them, do not use them.

Menu Planning

Serves: 2 people

Serves Well With:
- Pasta of Choice (I love to use Linguine or Fettuccine)
- Garlic Bread (p.50)

TIMELINE

Prep Time	25 minutes
Cook Time	+ 15 minutes
Total Time to Serving	**40 minutes**

INGREDIENTS

Measurement	Ingredient	Special Instructions/Notes
4 oz (about ¼ box)	Linguine or Fettuccine pasta	
1 Tbsp. + 2 Tbsp.	Extra Virgin Olive Oil	1 Tbsp for prepping the pasta, 2 Tbsp for making the sauce
1 Tbsp.	Fresh garlic	Chopped
⅛ tsp.	Red pepper flakes (optional)	
1 C. / 2 sticks	Salted butter	
1 Tbsp.	All-purpose flour	You may substitute almond flour to make gluten-free
⅓ C.	White wine or vegetable broth	
6 oz	Canned baby clams	
6	Fresh littleneck clams (optional)	See "Before You Get Started" on how to properly clean the clams
1 Tbsp. (plus more for garnish)	Fresh basil	Chopped

EQUIPMENT

Name of Equipment	Special Instructions/Notes
8 qt. stockpot	For cooking pasta
11-inch wok or 12-inch skillet with 2-inch sides and a lid	

DIRECTIONS

Step 1

Put a large pot of water on the stove, add a generous amount of salt, and bring to a boil. If you're using linguine, cook the pasta for 8 minutes, or follow the directions on the box, then drain. After draining, put 1 Tbsp olive oil in the pasta and toss to prevent the noodles from sticking together. While the water is coming to a boil and the pasta is cooking, you may begin to make the clam sauce.

Step 2

In a saute pan large enough to fit both pasta and sauce, add the olive oil over medium heat. Add the garlic and crushed red pepper and cook until golden brown, 2 minutes. Then add the butter and whisk the flour. Continue to whisk for 3 minutes. If the butter starts to brown, turn the heat down.

Step 3

Add the wine or broth, and the canned clams with all the juice, simmer for a few minutes. Check the sauce for your desired consistency- if the sauce is too thin, add a little more flour with a whisk. If the sauce is too thick, add a little more wine or broth. If you're using fresh clams, add them to the pan and top with a lid. Allow the clams to steam and cook until all the clams have opened, about 5 minutes. Add crushed red pepper if you like a little spice.

Step 4

When the clams have all opened you can put your pasta in the skillet and toss to coat. Plate your pasta and sauce, top with steamed clams and sprinkle with basil.

Buon appetito!

Linguine with Red Clam Sauce

This red clam sauce is made up of Villa Vespa Marinara Sauce, sauteed garlic, canned baby clams, and basil. I love to serve this over a bed of linguine with a side of garlic bread to soak up all the extra sauce. Adding the fresh littleneck clams makes it a little extra special. A delicious and easy little dinner.

Before You Get Started

- A few notes on clams- When you're dealing with canned clams, make sure to open and smell the can before using. It should not smell like anything.

- To clean the fresh clams before using- make sure to submerge them in a big bowl of cold salted water and let them soak for at least 5 minutes. This will help them to expel any remaining sand. Then scoop them out with a slotted spoon or fine mesh sieve, so you don't pour the sand back on top of them.

- Lastly, if the clams are open when you purchase them, do not use them.

Menu Planning

Serves: 2 people

Serves Well With:

- Pasta of Choice (I prefer linguine but you may use any pasta you like)
- Garlic Bread (p.50)
- Spinach Alla Villa Vespa (p.53)

TIMELINE

Prep Time	10 minutes (not including time to make the Villa Vespa Marinara Sauce)
Cook time	+ 20 minutes
Total Time to Serving	**30 minutes**

INGREDIENTS

Measurement	Ingredient	Special Instructions/Notes
¼ lb.	Dry Linguine	Imported Italian (such as De Cecco or Colavita)
1 Tbsp + 3 Tbsp.	Extra virgin olive oil	1 Tbsp for prepping the pasta, 3 Tbsp for making the sauce
1 Tbsp.	Fresh garlic	Chopped
1 ½ C.	Villa Vespa Marinara Sauce	Recipe on page 13
6oz	Can of baby clams	
6	Fresh littleneck clams (optional)	See "Before You Get Started" at the top of this recipe for instructions on how to properly clean the clams
¼ C.	Fresh basil	Chopped or julienned
⅛ tsp.	Red pepper flakes (optional)	

EQUIPMENT

Name of Equipment	Special Instructions/Notes
8 qt. stockpot	
11-inch wok or 12-inch skillet with 2-inch sides and a lid	

DIRECTIONS

Step 1

Put an 8-quart stockpot of water on the stove, add a generous amount of salt, and bring to a boil. If you're using linguine, cook the pasta for 8 minutes, or follow the directions on the box, then drain. Put 1 Tbsp olive oil in pasta and toss to prevent the noodles from sticking together. While the water is coming to a boil and the pasta is cooking, you may begin to make the clam sauce.

Step 2

In a wok or skillet large enough to fit both the pasta and the sauce, heat the olive oil over medium heat. Add garlic and cook for 3 minutes, until lightly brown. Next, add in the Villa Vespa Marinara Sauce.

Step 3

Pour ½ can of the clam juice into sauce. Do not use the whole can of juice or the sauce will be too watery. Discard the remainder of the juice and add the clams, cooking for 5 minutes. Turn the heat down to medium-low. If you are using fresh clams, add them to the pan, then top with a lid and steam the clams until they have all opened, about 5 minutes. Finish the sauce by adding in the fresh basil.

Step 4

Add the cooked pasta to the sauce and toss to coat the pasta. Add the red pepper flakes if you like a little spice.

Buon appetito!

Seafood Marinara

A mixture of fresh seafood simmered in Villa Vespa marinara sauce and fresh basil. I love that this is an impressive, one-skillet dinner. You will use this recipe over and over again.

Menu Planning

Serves: 4 people

Serves Well With:
- Pasta of choice (I recommend linguini)
- Garlic Bread (p.50)

Prep Time		15 minutes
Cook Time	+	30 minutes
Total Time to Serving		**45 minutes**

INGREDIENTS

Measurement	Ingredient	Special Instructions/Notes
3 Tbsp	Extra virgin olive oil	
1 Tbsp	Garlic	Chopped
4 C.	Villa Vespa Marinara Sauce	Recipe on page 13
4 8-oz	Haddock fillets	
8	Fresh littleneck clams	
16	Fresh mussels (optional)	
8	Jumbo Shrimp 16-20/lb	Raw & Cleaned (shell removed and deveined)
8	Sea Scallops	
1 C.	Squid (optional)	Cut in 2-inch rings
1 Tbsp	Fresh basil	Chopped
½ C.	White Wine (optional)	
1 pinch	Crushed red pepper (optional)	

EQUIPMENT

Name of Equipment	Special Instructions/Notes
Large saute pan with 4-6 inch sides and lid	

DIRECTIONS

Step 1

First clean the shrimp. To remove the tail, use a small paring knife and slice the shell off, being careful not to slice the shrimp. Next, butterfly the shrimp by making an incision on the back halfway through. This way, the shrimp will open up when cooking.

Step 2

Place a large saute pan on the stove over medium-heat and add olive oil to the pan. Toss in garlic and cook until lightly brown, about 3 minutes. Stir in the marinara sauce and bring to a simmer.

Step 3

Add the haddock, cook for 5 minutes. Add fresh clams and mussels. Place a lid on the pan to steam the shellfish, about 5 minutes.

Step 4

When the clams and mussels have opened, carefully place shrimp, scallops, and squid in the pan. Toss in fresh basil. Replace the lid on the pan and cook for 5 minutes. Add a splash of white wine, and simmer an additional 3 minutes, to ensure seafood is fully cooked. Sprinkle in crushed red pepper.

Step 5

To serve, first place a haddock fillet in each individual bowl or plate. Arrange the shellfish on top of haddock. Next, top the shellfish with the shrimp and scallops. Finally, mix the sauce gently and ladle it on top of the seafood. Serve with garlic bread or over a bed of pasta.

Buon appetito!

Shrimp Marinara

A classic Italian dish that is both easy and impressive if you're throwing a dinner party. It's even easier when your marinara sauce is made ahead of time. In the recipe below I've included directions for serving it with pasta, but it's just as good served over risotto.

Menu Planning

Serves: 4 people

Serves Well With:
- Pasta of Choice (I recommend Linguine or Fettuccine)
- Risotto Milanese (p.98)
- Haricots Verts w/ Roasted Peppers and Garlic (p. 56) or Spinach Alla Villa Vespa (p.53)

TIMELINE

Prep Time		40 minutes (Does not include time to make Villa Vespa Marinara Sauce)
Cook Time	+	25 minutes
Total Time to Serving		**1 hours, 5 minutes**

INGREDIENTS

Measurement	Ingredient	Special Instructions/Notes
20	Jumbo Shrimp 16-20/lb	Raw & Cleaned (shell removed and deveined)
½ lb.	Spaghetti or Linguini	
¼ C.	Extra Virgin Olive Oil	
2 Tbsp.	Fresh garlic	Chopped
1 tsp.	Crushed Red Pepper / Red Pepper Flakes (optional)	
3 C.	Villa Vespa Marinara Sauce	Recipe on page 13
¼ C.	Fresh basil	Chopped
1 tsp.	Salt	
1 tsp.	Pepper	

EQUIPMENT

Name of Equipment	Special Instructions/Notes
6-8-quart stock pot	For cooking the pasta
12-inch saute pan	

DIRECTIONS

Step 1

First clean the shrimp. To remove the tail, use a small paring knife and slice the shell off, being careful not to slice the shrimp. Next, butterfly the shrimp by making an incision on the back halfway through. This way, the shrimp will open up when cooking.

Step 2

Place a large pot of water on the stove with a generous amount of salt. Bring the water to a boil and cook the pasta according to the directions on the box or package. After draining the pasta, keep it warm, adding a splash of olive oil to prevent it from sticking together.

Step 3

Place a 12-inch saute pan over medium-high and add the olive oil. Once the oil has warmed, add the shrimp, one piece at a time. Make sure you have space in-between them so they will cook evenly. Cook for 3 minutes on the first side.

Step 4

When turning shrimp over to cook on the other side, add the garlic, and cook for another 3 minutes, allowing the garlic to become golden brown. Add crushed red pepper if you like a little spice.

Step 5

Next add the marinara sauce, basil, salt, and pepper to the saute pan and let it simmer until the shrimp is white in color, about 5 minutes.

Step 6

Transfer the pasta to your plates. Place shrimp on top of the pasta, then add top with the sauce.

Buon appetito!

Grilled Salmon with Creamy Dill Sauce

This was a special that we ran at the restaurant during the International Horseshow held in Lake Placid every summer. Although this is a fairly easy recipe to make, it is absolutely delicious and would make an elegant meal if you were hosting a dinner party.

Before You Get Started

Prepare the creamy dill sauce at least 10 minutes before the fish is done cooking, or up to two days ahead. If you're making the sauce ahead of time, store it in the fridge. Gently heat it up in a saucepan just before serving.

Menu Planning

Serves: 4 people

TIMELINE

Prep Time	15 minutes
Cook Time	+ 30 minutes
Total Time to Serving	45 minutes

INGREDIENTS

Measurement	Ingredient	Special Instructions/Notes
24-30 stalks	Asparagus (or green beans)	
4 Tbsp.	Butter	
1 tsp.	Flour	
½ C.	Sour Cream	
1	Large lemon	Halved; one half juiced, the other half sliced into rounds for garnish
2 Tbsp.	Fresh Dill	Finely chopped
1 tsp.	Garlic powder	
2 Tbsp.	Heavy Cream	
	Olive oil	For brushing the pan or grill and coating the fish
4 6oz	Salmon fillets	Skin on or off
	Parsley	

EQUIPMENT

Name of Equipment	Special Instructions/Notes
10-12-inch saucepan	
1-quart saucepan	
Cast-iron skillet, heavy pan, or a grill	

DIRECTIONS

Step 1

To prepare the asparagus, first cut one inch off the bottoms and discard. Using a vegetable peeler, peel the bottom of remaining stems to prevent toughness. Place water in a 10-12-inch saucepan, 2-inches deep, and add a pinch of salt. Heat the water until simmering then add the asparagus and steam for 5 minutes.

Step 2

To make the dill sauce, melt the butter In a small 1-quart saucepan over medium-low heat. When the butter is fully melted, whisk in 1 tsp flour. Continue to whisk for 3 minutes. Add the sour cream, juice of ½ lemon, fresh dill, and garlic powder. Stir to incorporate all the ingredients and continue to mix while slowly adding in the heavy cream. If the consistency is too thick, you may add 2 Tbsp water. Set the sauce off to the side while you cook the fish.

Step 3

Heat the cast-iron skillet, heavy pan, or grill, and add a touch of oil to the bottom or brush the grates of the grill with oil. Place the pan over medium-high heat. Rub both sides of the salmon with oil. Wait until the pan gets hot before cooking the fish, or it will stick to the pan. When it is hot enough, place the fish in the pan, skin side up. Cook 5-7 minutes, then turn the fish 45 degrees to make criss cross marks. Cook 5 minutes more. Turn the fish over to the other side and cook for 5 minutes more. Remove the fish from the pan and place on a cutting board or plate. Peel off the skin- it should come off easily.

Step 4

To assemble the plates, first pour ½ C. of the sauce onto each plate. Place the fish and vegetables on top and garnish with the sliced lemon and parsley. Finish with salt and serve with more sauce as needed.

Buon appetito!

Seafood Lasagna

A unique take on the classic lasagna. Layers of pasta, creamy bechamel, fresh seafood, sauteed vegetables, a light base of marinara, and a sprinkle of mozzarella come together for a casserole like no other. The amount of shrimp and scallops you put in is really a personal preference. It does not have to be exact so feel free to modify the quantities as you see fit.

Menu Planning

Serves: 6-8 people

Serves Well With:
- Side salad dressed with Balsamic Vinaigrette (p.72)
- Garlic Bread (p.50)

Prep Time	40 minutes (not including the time to make sauces)
Cook Time	35 minutes
Cool Time	+ 20 minutes
Total Time to Serving	**1 hour, 35 minutes**

EQUIPMENT

Name of Equipment	Special Instructions/Notes
8 x 10 x 2 inch oven/casserole pan	
2 8-inch saute pans	You can also use one pan- after making the vegetable mixture, just reserve it in a bowl and reuse pan to make the seafood mixture

INGREDIENTS

Measurement	Ingredient	Special Instructions/Notes
3 C.	Bechamel Sauce	Recipe on page 20
5 C.	Villa Vespa Marinara sauce	Recipe on page 13
⅓ C. + 1 Tbsp.	Olive oil	
1	Small onion	Diced
1 ½	Sweet red bell peppers	For the one bell pepper, seeded and diced (this will go in the vegetable mixture); For the half, seeded and cut into thin strips (this will be garnish at the end, just before baking)
1	Small zucchini	Peeled and diced
1 Tbsp. + ¼ C.	Fresh garlic	Chopped, (1 Tbsp in Vegetable Mixture, ¼ C. used for Seafood Mixture)
4 C.	Fresh spinach	Steamed in water with 1 tsp. Salt, then liquid squeezed out of it
1 tsp.	Salt	
1 tsp.	Pepper	
1 ½ lbs.	Shrimp	51/60 count, shell-off, patted dry with paper towels
1 ½ lbs.	Bay scallops (small scallops)	Patted dry with paper towels
10 oz.	Canned baby clams	Drained of water
2 Tbsp.	Butter	
1 Tbsp.	Flour	
¼ C.	Fresh basil	Chopped
	Oil Spray (such as Pam)	
18 oz.	Oven-ready lasagna noodles	I purchase 2 9-ounce boxes
16 oz.	Shredded mozzarella cheese	

DIRECTIONS

Step 1

Make the Bechamel Sauce (p.20), and Villa Vespa Marinara Sauce (p.13), according to their individual recipes. Set each aside until ready to assemble the lasagna.

Step 2

Preheat the oven to 350 degrees.

Step 3

Assemble the vegetable layer- in a medium saute pan over medium heat add ⅓ C. olive oil. Add the onions, red bell pepper, and zucchini, cook for 5 minutes, stirring. Then add the garlic, cook for 5 minutes more, stirring so the garlic does not brown. Add the cooked spinach, salt, and pepper. Stir all ingredients together, then take off the heat and set aside.

Step 4

Make the seafood layer- Either transfer the vegetable mixture to a bowl and reuse the saute pan, or place another pan on the burner. Add 1 Tbsp. olive oil over medium heat. Then, add the shrimp and scallops and cook for 5 minutes. Next add ¼ C. garlic and cook for 3 minutes more, or until the garlic is golden brown. Add the can of baby clams, drained of all water. Next add the butter. Once it melts, sprinkle in the flour and whisk for 5 minutes. Add the basil and set aside to cool.

Step 5

To assemble the lasagna, grease the bottom of the casserole pan with olive oil spray or butter. Add all the Villa Vespa Marinara Sauce to the base (there will be a lot). Add a layer of lasagna noodles, about 4.5 ounces or ¼ of all the pasta. For the next layer, add all the vegetable mixture and top with the shredded mozzarella. Add 2 layers of pasta, about 9 ounces- I add extra here to create a thicker middle. For the next layer, add the seafood mixture. Add a final pasta layer, about 4.5 ounces. Then, add a layer of Bechamel sauce and spread over the top. Garnish the top with the remaining bell pepper half that has been cut into thin strips. Lay the strips criss-cross all over the top.

Buon appetito!

Sweets

Amy's Pumpkin Bread

This recipe was given to me by Amy Beaney, who worked alongside me at the takeout shop. In my humble opinion, it is THE best pumpkin bread out there, in addition to being super easy!

Menu Planning

Makes: 3 Loaves

Serves Well With:
- A glass of milk
- A cup of coffee

TIMELINE

Prep Time		15 minutes
Bake Time		1 hour
Cooling Time	+	20 minutes
Total Time to Serving		**1 hours, 35 minutes**

INGREDIENTS

Measurement	Ingredient	Special Instructions/Notes
3 C.	Sugar	
3 ½ C.	Flour	
2 tsp.	Baking soda	
1 tsp.	Baking powder	
1 ½ tsp.	Salt	
¾ tsp.	Cinnamon	
¾ tsp.	Nutmeg	
¾ tsp.	Allspice	
¼ tsp	Ground cloves	
4	Eggs	
1 C.	Canola/vegetable oil or plain yogurt	I prefer oil because it results in a moister bread
⅔ C.	Water	
1 1lb	Canned Pumpkin puree	
1 C.	Walnuts (optional)	

EQUIPMENT

Name of Equipment	Special Instructions/Notes
3 8x4 loaf pans	Oiled/greased and floured

DIRECTIONS

Step 1

First, oil and flour the loaf pans and set them aside. In a large bowl, combine the sugar, flour, baking soda, baking powder, salt, cinnamon, nutmeg, allspice, and cloves.

Step 2

Add the eggs, oil or yogurt, water, and pumpkin puree. Mix well. Fold in the walnuts, if using.

Step 3

Pour mixture into the loaf pans, and bake 50-60 minutes. The middle should be cooked through. You can test the doneness by inserting a toothpick into the center. If it comes out dry, it is done. Let the loaves cool, about 20 minutes, then turn the pans over and the loaves will fall out. Slice and enjoy!

Buon appetito!

White Chocolate Holiday Bark

Thin pieces of white chocolate, filled with cranberries, sliced almonds, shredded coconut, and rice krispies. I found this recipe in Healthy Living back in 2008 and have been making it ever since. It makes a wonderful holiday gift. We sold an enormous number of beautifully wrapped bags at the Villa Vespa takeout store. One word of warning- these are highly addictive and it is very difficult to eat just one piece!

Before You Get Started

Make sure you use good, quality chocolate or it won't melt properly. Don't allow the heat to go above medium-high, or it will begin to seize.

Menu Planning

Makes: 30 servings

Serves Well With:
• A good cup of coffee

TIMELINE

Prep Time	15 minutes
Cook Time	8 minutes
Chill Time	+ 1 hour
Total Time to Serving	**1 hour and 23 minutes**

INGREDIENTS

Measurement	Ingredient	Special Instructions/Notes
1 C.	Sliced almonds	
¼ C.	Unsweetened Coconut	
1 C.	Rice Krispie cereal	
1 C.	Dried cranberries	
1 ½ lb.	Good quality white chocolate	Chopped or in rounds
2 tsp.	Vegetable oil	

EQUIPMENT

Name of Equipment	Special Instructions/Notes
Parchment Paper	
2 Baking sheets	
Double boiler or metal bowl set in a medium saucepan	

DIRECTIONS

Step 1

Preheat the oven to 350 degrees. Line the baking sheets with parchment paper.

Step 2

Spread the almonds and coconut evenly on one of the baking sheets and put in the oven. Toast 5-8 minutes, or until golden brown. Remove from the oven and let cool.

Step 3

In a large bowl, combine almonds, coconut, rice cereal, and dried cranberries. Set aside.

Step 4

Put the white chocolate and vegetable oil in a double boiler or place in a metal bowl and set over a medium saucepan of simmering water. Stir the chocolate with a spatula until it has melted completely.

Step 5

Remove chocolate from the heat and fold in the almond mixture, reserving ½ C. of the mixture to sprinkle on top. Pour the chocolate mixture onto the second parchment lined baking sheet. For easy spreading, dip the spatula into the warm water from the double boiler. Wipe the water off of the spatula before spreading the top of the chocolate.

Step 6

Sprinkle the reserved toppings on top, and press them down lightly so they stick. Let sit for 1 hour in a cool place. Break bark into small pieces with your hands.

Buon appetito!

Traditional Biscotti

This is a wonderful traditional biscotti recipe. I love to dip it into a strong cup of coffee or serve it with a glass of wine for an after-dinner treat.

Before You Get Started

These biscotti will last for a long time because of the Anisette liquor. Wrap them tightly in plastic wrap or place in an airtight container.

Menu Planning

Makes: About 20 biscotti cookies

Serves Well With:
- A strong cup of coffee
- A nice glass of wine

TIMELINE

Prep Time	45 minutes
Cook Time	1 hour, 15 minutes
Cool Time	+ 50 minutes
Total Time to Serving	**2 hours, 50 minutes**

INGREDIENTS

Measurement	Ingredient	Special Instructions/Notes
½ C.	Almond slices	
¼ C.	Anise seed	
½ lb.	Butter	Slightly melted
1 C.	Sugar	
4 C.	Flour	
½ Tbsp.	Baking powder	
3	Eggs	
⅛ C.	Anisette liquor	*This anise flavored liquor can be found in liquor stores
1 Tbsp.	Water	
1 Tbsp.	Vanilla extract	
1 C.	Walnuts	Finely chopped

EQUIPMENT

Name of Equipment	Special Instructions/Notes
2 baking sheets	
Parchment paper	
Small saucepan (optional)	
Electric stand mixer	
Dough cutter (optional)	

DIRECTIONS

Step 1

Preheat the oven to 350 degrees. Once the oven has come to temperature, toast the almond slices and anise seed on a baking sheet for 10 minutes.

Step 2

Line a baking sheet with parchment paper. Using either a small saucepan or microwavable bowl Melt the butter just slightly, using either a small saucepan on the stove or in a bowl in the microwave.

Step 3

Using an electric stand mixer, slowly mix the sugar, flour, and baking powder together.

Step 4

In a large bowl, combine the butter, eggs, anisette, water, and vanilla extract and mix until everything is well blended. Pour the wet ingredients into the mixing bowl with the dry ingredients.

Add the walnuts, almond slices, and anise seed. Mix together at low speed until well combined. The dough should come together nicely.

Step 5

Remove the dough from the bowl and turn out onto a floured cutting board. Cut the dough in half (if you have a dough cutter, this makes this job easier). Using one of the dough halves, form a long narrow log of dough. Repeat with the second. Press the tops of the logs down to smooth and flatten.

Step 6

Put both halves on the parchment lined baking sheet and bake in the oven for 25 minutes.

Step 7

After you remove the pan from the oven, allow it to cool completely, about 30 minutes.

Step 8

Transfer the cooled biscotti to a cutting board. Using a sharp bread knife, slice the biscotti horizontally into ¾-inch slices. Be gentle so they do not break.

Step 9

Once you've sliced all the biscotti, put a new piece of parchment paper on the baking sheet and place the sliced biscotti next to each other, 1 inch apart.

Step 10

Once you've laid out all the biscotti on the baking sheet, put it back in the oven to bake for 20 minutes more. Allow to cool completely, about 20 minutes, then enjoy!

Buon appetito!

Grandma Eaton's Peanut Butter Balls

I am estimating this recipe to be at least 70 years old. I received it as a present from the granddaughter of Grandma Eaton at a cookie exchange party. We packaged these tiny treats in beautiful little boxes and sold them during the holidays at the takeout store. Thank you Kimmy Cohen!

Before You Get Started

Since you will be rolling and dipping 80 balls, my suggestion when making this recipe would be to grab some friends and make it a party! You can cut this recipe in half, but if you're making them as holiday gifts, this is a perfect quantity.

Menu Planning

Makes: About 80 balls

TIMELINE

Prep Time		2 hours
Cook Time	+	15 minutes
Total Time to Serving		**2 hour, 15 minutes**

INGREDIENTS

Measurement	Ingredient	Special Instructions/Notes
1 lb.	Creamy peanut butter	
½ lb.	Butter (do not substitute)	Softened, do not melt
1 ½ lb.	Confectioners sugar	
24 oz	Semi-sweet chocolate chips or chocolate disks	Good quality chocolate

EQUIPMENT

Name of Equipment	Special Instructions/Notes
3 baking sheet sheets	
Parchment paper	Enough to cover 3 baking sheets
Disposable gloves	
½ ounce melon baller with hand release like an ice cream scooper	
Double-boiler or 4-quart saucepan with a metal bowl that fits snugly on top (so it does not fall in)	
½ box canning wax	Canning wax was a wax used in the old days to seal jam jars. It can be found in the baking section of any grocery store next to the canning jars or pectin. The wax gives the chocolate a nice shine and helps holds the shine.
Long toothpicks	

DIRECTIONS

Step 1

First, line the baking sheets with parchment paper. Using a spatula, mix the peanut butter and the melted butter together in a large bowl. Switch to a spoon and slowly begin adding the sugar a little at a time, stirring in-between adding to gradually incorporate the sugar into the mixture. When it becomes too difficult to stir with the spoon, use disposable gloves to begin mixing it by hand. Continue to mix until all the sugar has disappeared into the peanut butter, and it is soft and pliable.

Step 2

Using a melon baller, scoop the mixture onto one of the parchment lined baking sheets. After the entire mixture has been scooped, roll each peanut butter ball by hand to make them smooth and round.

Step 3

Place either a double-boiler or a 4-quart saucepan on the stove over medium heat. Add 4 inches of water to the pot and bring to a simmer. If using the saucepan, place a metal bowl on top, it should be a large enough bowl that it does not fall in. To the double boiler or metal bowl, add the canning wax and allow it to melt.

Step 4

Add all the chocolate into the melted wax and begin stirring as the chocolate begins to melt. Do not let the water come to a boil. Continue to stir until the chocolate has melted. Remove the double boiler or pot from the heat to begin dipping the peanut butter balls into the chocolate. The water below will keep chocolate melted for some time. If the chocolate starts to thicken, place the double boiler or pan back onto the stove and stir to melt again.

Step 5

Using a long toothpick, pierce into a peanut butter ball, then tip into the chocolate until it is completely covered. Hold the dipped ball over the bowl and let the excess drip off. Gently lay it onto a new parchment lined tray to dry. Repeat with all the remaining balls. When the chocolate has dried, you may pull out the toothpick. You may use the toothpicks more than once. The chocolate will take about 15 minutes to harden.

Buon appetito!

CPSIA information can be obtained
at www.ICGtesting.com
Printed in the USA
LVHW071732100322
713133LV00006B/194

9 781662 920608